The Art of DRIED AND PRESSED FLOWERS

Pamela Westland has worked in magazine and book publishing all her life — even when she was still at school, she says. Having edited a woman's magazine for six years, she now works from her home, an old farmhouse in Essex where she lives with her husband and six cats. Her main interests, besides work, are interior decorating, architecture, archaeology, cooking, travelling in Greece, and cats. She is also the author of The Complete Home Crafts Book.

Paula Critchley studied at the Chelsea School of Art in London and holds the National Diploma of Design for illustration work. She holds weekend art classes and has for many years been an enthusiastic collector of shells. She is the author of The Art of Shellcraft.

The Art of
DRIED AND
PRESSED FLOWERS

Pamela Westland and Paula Critchley

Pan Books

London and Sydney

First published in Great Britain 1974 by
Ward Lock Ltd
This edition published 1975 by Pan Books Ltd,
Cavaye Place, London SW10 9PG
5th printing 1983
ISBN 0 330 24374 8
(c) Pamela Westland 1974

Designed by Paula Hawkins

Drawings by Paula Critchley

Pages 58 and 64 designed by Micky Scammell

Printed by Cripplegate Printing Co, Ltd. Edenbridge, Kent.

Acknowledgments
The publishers acknowledge with thanks the
permission of the copyright owners to
reproduce Eleanor Farjeon's poem, 'The
Clove Orange' from her book, Silver Sand
and Snow, published by Michael Joseph
Limited.

Contents

Chapter 1

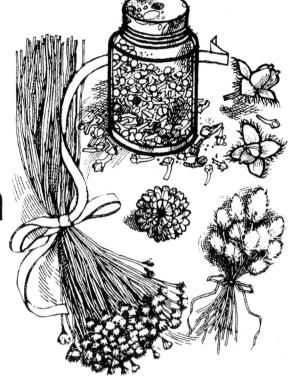

Introduction

THE ART OF DRIED AND PRESSED FLOWERS is the art of extending the life of natural plant materials of all kinds; the art of recognising the beauty and charm of leaves, seedheads and pods which are often overshadowed when the plant is in bloom.

Nature does much of the work for us. Some flowers dry colourfully and perfectly in the garden; seedheads dry on the stem like a second flowering, and grasses and cereals, crisp and dry, need very little attention after picking. In many cases, harvesting the materials before they have completely dried on the plant is simply a matter of keeping them indoors under controlled conditions and not risking spoilage by unfavourable weather.

So much stress has been laid on the problems of drying and preserving plant materials, that there are people who, quite understandably, come to regard the process as a science more than an art. This is a pity, because it is just not so. A very large and varied collection can be built up of materials which need no more attention than tying in bunches and hanging upside down in a warm, airy place; standing loosely in a container, or being laid flat on a cardboard box lid. This category covers the grasses, seedpods, seedheads and even some flowers—the everlastings—which you will find in the designs throughout this book.

Preserving leaves, hips and some berry fruits on the stem is very little more trouble; simply a matter of heating a water and glycerine solution and leaving the stems immersed in it for a number of days or weeks. This process opens up another whole range of plant materials which will last practically for ever and reward you with colours often deeper and richer than those on the plant. Herbs such as rosemary, berry fruits such as blackberry, and rowan berries and rose hips can be preserved on the stem for glistening and glowing winter and Christmas decorations. Large single leaves like maple, sprays of leaves like beech or oak can all be treated in this way and then used in arrangements or flat picture designs.

To extend the range of dried flowers in your collection beyond the colourful everlastings—rhodanthe, helipterum, helichrysum and so on—you need nothing more complicated than an airtight container and a granular or powdered compound such as treated sand, household borax or silica gel crystals. And the patience to handle delicate materials carefully!

When the moment comes to ease away the compound, it is as exciting as unwrapping a birthday present. For it is almost impossible to believe that your garden flowers will emerge with all the fullness and most of the colour they had when you picked them. Yellow flowers such as sprays of forsythia and clusters of tiny narcissus hold their colour particularly well; others do not fade so much as soften a little. In this way, you can gradually build up a collection of garden flowers that will brighten and enhance your home until the natural flowering season comes round again.

There will be no prizes for following the designs in this book, because they do not conform to the rules accepted by horticultural or flower clubs. They are a personal expression of a love for natural materials and, as such, a varied collection of ideas ranging from decorated pomanders and tight little posies of herbs to a lavish display in a watering can and a garland for an ornament.

The emphasis throughout the text is always on the mood and feeling of the design, and never on any individual flower or leaf. It does not matter, therefore, if you cannot obtain just the materials we have used; you will soon be able to understand the essence of what has been created and adapt it to suit your own collection. In every design, study the balance between round and flat shapes, strong and muted colours, hard and soft outlines, the proportion of natural materials to container, and then create your own shapes and patterns, your own expression of your personal love for flowers.

14

15

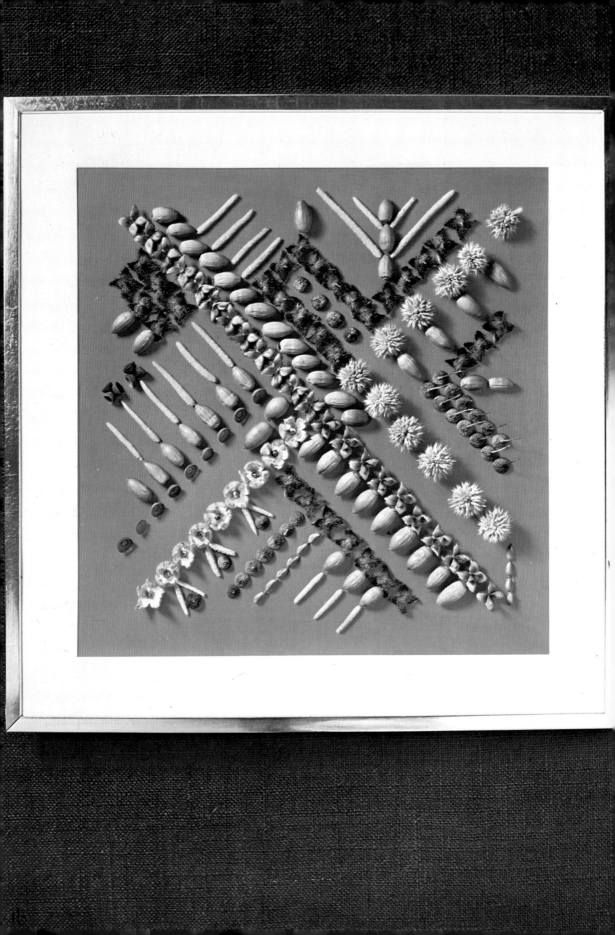

Chapter 2

How to Dry Natural Materials

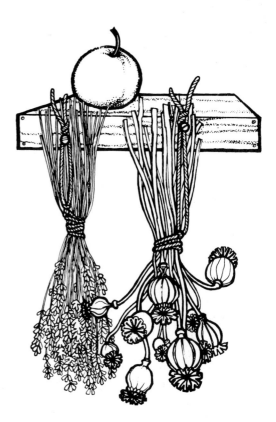

There is no cause for sadness at the end of a lovely season in the garden or countryside. It need not be the end of the mellow fruitfulness, but a new beginning. For practically every kind of plant material can be dried in some form. The leaves, which are usually pressed, the flowers and the seedheads, will all be happy practically ever after in arrangements and other designs in the home.

Many cultivated and wild flowers change very little after being dried in a chemical substance. They retain their natural shape and form so convincingly that sometimes one has actually to touch them to be sure they are not fresh. These dried flowers feel crisp and papery to the touch, as crumpled tissue paper does, and fade slightly, like antique velvet. It is almost as if the sun has drawn out a little of the colour, leaving them with softer, more muted tones.

Dried grasses and corn retain almost all of their natural characteristics, and in mid-winter evoke welcome memories of slanting sunlight on golden fields. They provide a wide variety of shape and texture, some upright and soldierly, others drooping into cloudy outlines. The pale creamy golden colours of so many dried grasses are invaluable in designs of all kinds, providing as they do a nearly neutral hue against which other colours are shown to their best advantage.

The study of seedheads, which quickly becomes second nature to a flower arranger, is a fascinating one in itself. Many plants have what is virtually a second flowering season in the form of seed capsules, delicate and delightful shapes, subtle and pleasing colours which have only to be hung upside down or stood in a container to dry. This valuable material, which is all too often consigned to the compost heap by the unknowing, is easy to come by. No-one minds asking friends for something that was going to be thrown away, and a varied collection can soon be built up.

When to harvest

As with farmers, so with flower arrangers: conditions have to be just right for harvest. Ideally, all plant material for drying should be gathered on a dry day, after the morning dew has evaporated in the sun. But since you will be harvesting from the early spring – for the seed capsules of the small species bulbs – to the late autumn and even beyond, and since this is not an ideal world, you will have to gather material as and when you can. It is better to capture a basketful of seedheads which are not quite ready than to watch the next storm batter them to the ground.

If you have to collect rain-soaked plant material, shake it gently and lay it on sheets of blotting or newspaper, turning it over until all the excess moisture has been absorbed.

Everlasting flowers such as acroclinium, rhodanthe and helichrysum should be cut just as the flowers open. A patch of these annuals sown at the same time will need daily scrutiny. The flowers will develop at a different rate and be ready a few each day.

Long spikes of flowers, such as delphinium, should be cut before some of the topmost buds open. This is not only the stage at which they will dry most successfully, but captures the flower at its most interesting, with the widest variety of shape, texture and colour. Other flowers should be cut just as they are about to open. This means keeping daily watch. Thistles, bulrushes and pampas grass, which disintegrate so easily, need to be cut even before this stage, when they are only half developed.

Seedheads will dry naturally on the plant and indeed can be left to do so. However, it is safer to bring them in and dry them under controlled conditions than to risk a bad spell of weather.

A free circulation of air round the drying plant material is recommended, and so hanging upside down or standing in containers is usually best. In some cases, material can be dried flat on box-lids, but it should be turned occasionally.

Any dry, dark, airy room is suitable – a spare bedroom, boxroom, garden room or garage or even, as in the colour photograph on page 9, an old chimney corner. Slow drying causes fading; warmth and dark are essential for the best results. Large spikes of delphinium need more warmth, such as an airing cupboard.

Remove the leaves first. They do not dry well by this method, and only serve to increase the moisture content of the room as they do so. The leaves need not be discarded, though – they can be dried by pressing (Chapter 3).

Hang-drying

Tie flowers and seedheads in bunches according to type. The stems will shrink as the material dries and the cord or twine will need to be tightened to prevent flowers and seedheads from falling to the floor. Use gardeners' twine or raffia – not coarse string – and tie a slip knot which can be pulled tighter without being untied and retied. Very fine and delicate stems should be tied with silk thread, split raffia or gardeners' ties.

Suitable material for hang-drying
Acanthus or Bear's Breeches (*Acanthus species*) Hardy perennial   Dry the tall sweeping

arcs of pink, white and mauve flower heads in a warm room. Good for designs where height is needed – arrangements on the floor or pedestals, in churches, halls and so on.

Achillea or Yarrow (*Achillea species*) Hardy perennial   Flowers can be dried upside down or upright in containers. Many wild and cultivated species from dwarf forms to a height of 4–5 feet. Pick when flower heads are young.

Acroclinium (*Helipterum*) Half-hardy annual   An everlasting flower in yellow, white and pink. Grows to a height of about 1 foot.

Allium   From the small, round clover-like flowers of the chive to A. Moly (garlic), which produces bright yellow umbrella-shaped flowers, these bulbous herbs are invaluable for flower design. Hang-dry chive flowers; dry the flowers of the garlic upright or flat. Onion heads, too, large balls of blue-mauve flowers, can be hang-dried. Too large for many arrangements, they go a long way in pictures or small arrangements if the star-shaped spikes are used separately.

Bells of Ireland (*Molucella laevis*) Half-hardy annual   Remove the leaves and dry the 18-inch spikes of olive green bells. They gradually become as stiff as paper cones and fade to a rich creamy parchment colour. Can also be preserved in glycerine.

Bluebell (*Scilla*)   Pick the heads when they are already becoming dry and papery and hang until the process is complete. Can also be dried upright in a container.

Bulrush   Grows in and around ponds and on marshy land. Pick the long, poker-straight spikes when they are half developed.

Burdock   The burrs of this plant, often a bristly and prickly irritant on a country walk, dry well and keep their colour.

Carrot   One of the few leaves dried successfully hanging upside down. Very useful to give softness to small designs.

Chinese Lanterns or Cape Gooseberry (*Physalis franchetii*) Hardy perennial   Dry the seedheads. Cut when the calyces have not all ripened. The pale coral and yellowy green colours of the not-quite-developed seedheads soften the somewhat overpowering effect of the deep orange. Use in sprays or snip off individual seedheads and use for dried-flower pictures or designs on pre-formed shapes (flower balls, cones, door wreaths and so on).

Clarkia Hardy annual   The white, pink and purple flowers dry extremely well and keep their colour. Can also be dried flat.

Clematis (*C. Vitalba* is known as Old Man's Beard or Traveller's Joy) Hardy perennial   These flowers give a good range of deep colour – strong mauve, purple and pink. If you do not cut the flowers in time to dry them, you have a second chance because many varieties have large, fluffy seedheads which dry well, too. These are often found growing wild in hedges.

Columbine (*Aquilegia*) Hardy perennial   Harvest the seedheads as soon as they open and start curving outwards, but not before.

Delphinium and Larkspur Hardy perennial and annual   Dry both flowers and seed-heads – a difficult choice to make. Pick flowers for drying when some buds are still unopened and dry in a heated room. Seedheads can also be dried flat.

Dock   Can be found in ditches and on waste land.
The whorl-shaped seedheads change from lime green to deep red when dried. Can also be preserved in glycerine.

Foxglove (*Digitalis*) Hardy annual, biennial and perennial   Can be found growing wild, or cultivated. Dry the seedheads which often grow in gently curving S shape. They can be used singly in small designs.

Glixia   These everlasting flowers, with minute star-like heads, can be bought dyed in bright colours. The honey, ginger brown and pale cream colours seem to complement other dried materials best, but some brighter ones are useful for accent.

Globe Artichoke (*Cynara scolymus*)   The huge purple flower heads, like great thistles, dry well and turn glistening cream.

Globe Thistle (*Echinops ritro*) Hardy perennial   Cut the steel-blue globular flower heads as they are just beginning to open. Leave them any longer and they will disintegrate as they dry. The Greek name means hedgehog – a warning that the flowers and stems are prickly to handle.

Golden Rod (*Solidago*) Hardy perennial   Dry the long flower spikes either hanging upside down or upright in a container. Cut stems in a range of sizes to give flexibility to arrangements; the largest are not always the most useful. Sprays of the laterals can be snipped off for small-scale designs.

Grasses   Some grasses can be dried by hanging upside down but most give more satisfactory results when flat-dried on trays or box lids (see Flat Drying). If there is any doubt about the stems being strong enough to hold the weight of the heads, then it is better to be safe and dry the material horizontally.

Heaths and Heathers (*Erica and Calluna*) Hardy shrubs   Pick the stems when the flowers have just opened. May be dried by hanging or upright in a little water. Some flowers turn an attractive brown, others stay white.

Helichrysum or Straw Daisies Half-hardy annual or half-hardy shrub   These everlasting flowers, in a wide range of colours from pale cream to deep burgundy, are among the most useful of dried plant material. Some arrangers recommend binding each stem with wire before drying. If the flowers are for use in arrangements where height is needed, this might be worth doing.

Hollyhock (*Althaea*) Hardy perennial   If you do not cut the flowers in time to preserve them, then you can dry the long stems of seedheads by hanging upside down or flat. Individual seedheads, each on a short stem, can be used in pictures and other designs where the plant material is used close to the surface – such as decorations based on foam cones and hoops.

Honesty (*Lunaria*) Hardy biennial   The dried silvery-moon seedpods have an ethereal, translucent quality. Cut the stems when the centre layer, like silver tissue-paper, is still protected by two brown outer skins. When you are ready to arrange the sprays, rub these layers off between thumb and first finger.

Hop (*Humulus*) Hardy annual   *H. Lupulus* is the common hop, often found twining round fences and poles and in hedges. It can be dried by hanging upside down or preserved in glycerine. The pale olive green flowers fade only slightly and the individual papery blossoms are useful in picture designs.

Larkspur See **Delphinium.**

Lavender (*Lavandula*) Hardy shrub   For drying, cut the stems before the flowers are fully open and hang upside down or leave in a little water without replenishing.

Love-in-a-Mist (*Nigella*) Hardy annual   Pretty as the pink, white or blue flowers are, one is reluctant to cut them and sacrifice the dramatic seedheads which are almost globular and vary from cream to reddish purple. Some are striped in those colours. Remove most of the frondy fennel-type leaves, but leave a few near the seedhead to frame it.

Lupin (*Lupinus*) Hardy perennial   Cut stems of varying length, some straight and some curved. The spikes of dried pea-pod-like seedheads give height and width to large arrangements; the pods can also be used individually in miniature designs.

Maize or Sweet Corn   When the cob has ripened and been cut, the long spikes of seedheads and the husk which enclosed the cob can be hung-dried. The husks take on the appearance of crepe paper and dry to a pale avocado green colour.

Mallow (*Lavatera*) Hardy annual   Pink or white flowers are replaced by pale silver-grey seedheads like closed-up stars.

Nipplewort (*Lapsana*)   A weed in the garden, it is not found in a seedsman's catalogue, but is highly valuable in arrangements. Gather as soon as the flowers are over and the seedheads beginning to open. Dry upside down or flat.

Onion (*Allium*)   Dry the large round seedheads.

Pampas Grass (*Cortaderia*) Hardy perennial   The huge, soft, feathery spikes, surely the most majestic of all grasses, should be cut before they start to shed. If this is not possible, they can be kept in shape by spraying with ordinary hair lacquer.

Poppy (*Papaver*) Hardy annual   All kinds of poppy, from the tiny ones found growing wild to the much larger cultivated varieties, provide excellent seedheads which are invaluable in any collection of dried material. And, since poppies last a relatively short time when cut, it seems almost an investment to allow the urn-shaped seedheads to develop. Harvest them throughout the summer and autumn, shaking out the black seeds for next year's crop.

Rhodanthe   Half-hardy annual   These pinky-white cone-shaped everlasting flowers retain their colour well when dried.

Russian Vine   Cut the flowers as soon as they open and hang in a dark room.

Sea Holly (*Eryngium*) Hardy perennial   Dry the pale blue, round flower heads on the stems, with the leaves.

Sea Lavender or Statice (*Limonium*) Hardy perennial   The small sprays of faded-lavender blue, pink or green everlasting flowers dry well and in arrangements give much the same effect as a passing, fluffy cloud.

Senecio Hardy annual and half-hardy shrub   The annual has loose clusters of red, pink, lilac or white flowers and the shrub, a creeper, yellow heads which flower in December. The flowers dry to a warm yellowy brown, the leaves silver on one side and sage green on the other.

Shoo-fly Plant (*Nicandra*) Hardy annual   Dry the apple-shaped fruits.

Smoke Tree (*Rhus*)   Dry the seedheads of this tree which live up to the name and, when dried, look like a puff of smoke and give a soft outline to a design.

Stonecrop (*Sedum*) Hardy perennial   Flowers dry to a subtle pinky-beige in soft sprays.

Sycamore   Any tree which produces seeds in the form of "keys" is worth watching. They should be cut before they are ripe and start floating down to the ground.

Teasel (*Dipsacus*) Hardy biennial   These long stems with seedheads like hairbrushes are often found on waste land. They dry so well that it is worth clambering over ditches and getting scratched to secure them.

Thistle (*Onopordon*) Hardy perennial   Scotch or Cotton thistles, with their intriguing and intricate formation, are exciting materials to use in dried plant designs.

Xeranthemum Hardy annual   Everlasting flowers with strong, wiry stems. Retain colour well after drying.

Flat drying

Smaller and more delicate materials can be dried flat on trays, box lids, in shallow boxes or on sheets of thick brown paper. Grasses, especially, take well to this treatment; follow this method if you judge that the stems would not be strong enough to support the weight of the heads when hanging upside down.

We dried most of the grasses on wooden racks, including hare's tail grass (*Lagurus*), squirrel grass (*Hordeum*), quaking grass (*Briza maxima*) and all the cereals—wheat, barley, oats and rye; the flowers of the hardy annual clarkia and allium (garlic) were dried flat on box lids, and the long spikes of delphinium, larkspur and hollyhock seedheads on sheets of brown paper on top of a wardrobe.

Gourds, ornamental (*Cucurbita*)   Dry in hot airing cupboard for 3 months. Paint with clear varnish.

Drying in water

Some materials respond well to drying by standing upright in a container with $\frac{1}{2}$–1 inch of water. Allow the material to absorb as much of the water as it will, but do not top it up. Try this method for hydrangea flower heads, lavender and all heaths and heathers and compare the results of another batch you have dried by hanging upside down. Results vary according to climatic and other conditions and so it is advisable to make these simple experiments for yourself and thereafter use the one which was most satisfactory.

Upright drying

To make the best use of the space, you can stand containers of upright-drying material beneath the ones that are hang-drying. Choose containers in scale with the size of the material; used preserve jars for the smallest stems and milk bottles, old plastic buckets, a length of drain pipe or even an old boot for the longest ones.

Suitable material for upright drying

Achillea or Yarrow   Flower heads can also be dried hanging upside down.

Allium (garlic)   Can also be dried flat.

Artichoke, globe   Strip off the leaves, run a sharp knife down the stems to remove the prickles and stand the large purple flower heads (picked when only half developed) in deep containers to dry.

Bluebell (*Scilla*)   Leave the stems on the plant until they have started to dry. Stand loosely in a wide container to allow free circulation of air round the heads.

Grape Hyacinth (*Muscari*)   As for Bluebell.

Giant Hogweed   This plant, which looks like overgrown rhubarb, is a vigorous grower. It has huge umbrella-shaped clusters of pale green seed pods which can be used in large arrangements or separated into tiny sprays for smaller designs. The heads are rather top heavy, so stand the hollow stems in a bucket filled with dry sand to anchor them while drying.

Golden Rod (*Solidago*) Hardy perennial   Can also be dried hanging upside down.

Honesty (*Lunaria*) Hardy biennial   Stand the stems in a wide container, or distribute into several. The papery seedpods are carried on long lateral shoots and the stems easily become intertwined. Rub off the two brown outside layers when the pods have dried, to reveal the silvery petal-like centres. Can also be dried upside down.

Lavender (*Lavandula*) Hardy shrub   Lavender flowers, picked before they are fully developed, can be dried upright, upside down, or in a container with a little water. Allow the water to be taken up, but do not replenish.

Pinks (*Dianthus*) Hardy perennial   Pick the flowers before they are fully open. To retain the natural colour, it is important to keep them in a dark place. Pinks can also be dried in desiccants.

Santolina or Lavender Cotton Hardy shrub   When dried, the tiny flower heads fade from bright yellow to yellowish brown.

Spiraea Hardy perennial   The white flowers of the variety Meadowsweet dry pale parchment colour.

Sweet William (*Dianthus*) Hardy biennial   Pick the flower heads just before they are fully open; they will dry into balls of muted coloured flowers.

Storing

As each batch of material dries—and you will recognise this stage more by the rustling sound it makes when you touch it than by any marked change in appearance—carefully cut the binding, if any, and gently shake the stems. Store where the heads will be least likely to be disturbed or get crushed. If you have the space, the ideal method is to push the stems into blocks of dry holding material, the heads upright and not touching each other. If not, choose the method that best suits your storage facilities: standing upright in containers, spread on crumpled tissue paper on racks or shelves, or packed carefully in boxes between layers of tissue. In any event keep dried material away from direct sunlight and in a dry room. The author found that the crispy, crackly quality of dried material attracted one of her cats, who enlisted a bucket of hydrangea heads as instant playthings, while another kitten found racks of hillocky tissue paper irresistible as a sleeping place.

Because of its brittle nature, you must handle dried material with special care at all times. If it does lose its shape, you can restore it by holding it for a few seconds over the jet of steam from a kettle. Twist the stem round so that each part of the head is exposed to the steam and then gently reshape the material.

Look carefully at all your dried material as you store it and try to visualise it in other ways. Some of the largest sprays offer rich potential for small designs and pictures once you are able to separate each individual seedpod or flower head in your imagination. A long spike of lupin seedpods, for example, is not immediately recognisable as one of the most attractive of assets. Yet it is composed of numerous silvery, furry pods, each on its own short stalk, which can be used in miniature arrangements or in pictures.

The long tapering spikes of golden rod are made up of many small flower sprays. You will probably want to strip off some of the lower ones when arranging the long stems, so save these for small-scale work.

The petals of dried hydrangea flowers are invaluable in picture designs; the small olive green hop flowers colourful and attractive when snipped off on a short length of stem; hare's tail grass, like little balls of fur, perfect for close work, such as the decorated pomanders in Chapter 9.

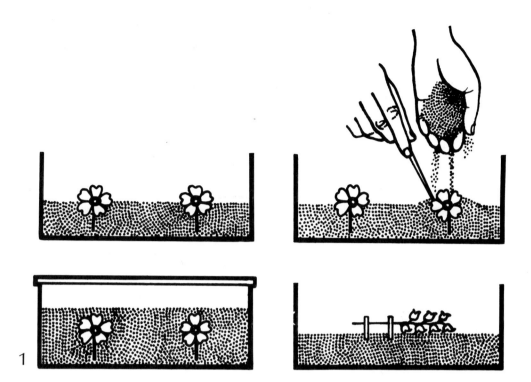

1

Drying in desiccants

Although some flowers can be dried successfully by the means described many more can be preserved in a desiccant. That is to say the flower is completely immersed in a material which gradually draws the moisture from it. All the flowers in the miniature arrangement shown in the colour photograph on page 57 were dried in this way. There is a slight deepening of the red, blue and violet colours and a slight fading of the others, but apart from that the flowers look entirely natural.

There are several different types of desiccant and the one you use might well depend on local availability. The lightest in weight, and therefore the most suitable for delicate flowers, is household borax, available in 1-lb. packs from chemists and hardware stores. This should not be confused with the medical quality of borax, which costs more. The principle when using borax, as with all other desiccants, is to cover the flower completely, shaking and working the material under, between and on top of all the petals so that there is not even a minute air pocket preventing the desiccant from coming into contact with the surface of the flower. Because of its lightness, borax is a little difficult to work into the flower and can be gently pushed into the cavities with a small camelhair paintbrush. It can be used with an equal quantity of cornmeal.

Sand is a readily absorbent material and has been used successfully to dry flowers for generations. However it needs thorough washing before it is ready to use. To do this, put the sand into a bucket, fill with water, stir well, and pour off the excess. Fill the bucket again, add a little household detergent, stir to distribute the cleaner, then pour off the water. Rinse the sand several times in fresh water, until finally the water poured away is clear. Spread out the sand on trays and dry in the sun or in the oven at a very low temperature. This will take 3–4 hours.

Sand is considerably heavier than household borax and will run freely and smoothly between the flower petals. Care should be taken to support the flower from underneath while this is being done, or the weight of the sand could be damaging.

Silica gel crystals are an effective desiccant, too. They are useful to prevent moisture from attacking metals; a few crystals kept in a camera case or tool box prevent rust. The crystals are rather large, however, and should be ground before being used to dry flowers. If you cannot buy ground silica gel crystals, you can easily crush them with a rolling pin. Since this material can absorb up to fifty per cent of its own weight in moisture, the granules must be dried before they are ready to use again. To do this, spread them in a baking tray in a low oven until the litmus paper indicator, sold with the substance for this purpose, turns blue.

Similar in effect to these crystals, is a desiccant called Cut 'N Keep, marketed by Readers Offer Limited of Oriel House, 2a Rectory Grove, Leigh-on-Sea, Essex, and available by post to readers in the U.K. and overseas. At the time of going to press, it costs £1·00 per tin, inclusive of U.K. postage. This substance comes in the form of fine dark blue crystals. After use, and depending on the amount of moisture absorbed, the crystals turn paler blue or, later, pink. To be reactivated, they need to be put in hot sun or a cool oven as described.

Whichever desiccant is used, the method is the same. Pour a layer of desiccant over the bottom of an airtight container, such as lidded polythene sandwich box, a cake tin or a large used coffee tin. Push the short stem of a flower into the material and, supporting the flower underneath with the fingers of one hand, gently and slowly pour on the desiccant, working it well in between the petals (Diagram 1). The success of the drying operation will depend on the care taken at this stage. If some of the petals are not completely covered, damp spots and eventually mildew will result. Add a second and third flower to the container, covering it in the same way, but making sure that it does not touch any other flower. Pour on a further 1½–2 inches of the desiccant and cover the box securely. If you are in any doubt about its airtight properties, stick a strip of self-adhesive tape round the rim of the lid. Move the container, very carefully, without tipping, to a place where it will not be disturbed and leave it for at least one day, or according to the type of flower being dried. The following table listing some of the flowers that can be dried in this way will be a guide to approximate drying times. The exact time will depend to a great extent on the size and moisture content of each flower and the temperature of the room. A dry warm room gives the best results. To test for readiness, slowly pour off the desiccant if there is only one flower in the box. If there are more, gently work your fingers under the desiccant and lift out one of the flowers, supporting it from below. Shake the material from the petals. They should feel as crisp as cornflakes and make a slight rustling sound when touched. If they do not, return the flower carefully, covering it completely again with the desiccant. Test again the next day.

When the flowers are ready to be removed, gently shake off the excess material by holding each one upside down. If any desiccant remains on the petals – borax is the most likely to adhere to the flower – brush it off carefully with a fine camelhair paintbrush.

Store the dried flowers by pushing the delicate stems carefully into dry holding material so that no two flowers are touching each other. Keep them in a dry room away from direct sunlight. To use dried flowers in arrangements and other designs where longer stems are needed, you can push the short stem into a longer dried one – a hollow-stemmed cereal for instance.

Flower	Type	Approximate number of days to dry	Notes
Broom (*Cytisus or Genista*)	Hardy shrub	2	Cut when not quite in full bloom. Lay short sprays flat. Retains both colour and shape well
Carnation (*Dianthus caryophyllus*)	Hardy perennial	4	Cut before fully in bloom
Daisy (*Bellis*)	Hardy perennial	4	Stems need wiring before drying
Forsythia	Hardy Shrub	2	Dry short sprays horizontally
Hyacinth		3	Stems need wiring
Laburnum	Hardy tree	2	As for Broom
Larkspur (*Delphinium*)	Hardy perennial	2–3	Dry small young shoots
Lilac (*Syringa*)	Hardy perennial	2	Dries very well
Lily of the Valley (*Convallaria*)	Hardy perennial	1	"Fades" to deep cream
London Pride (*Saxifraga umbrosa*)	Hardy perennial	2	Very useful shape
Marigold (*Calendula and Tagetes*)	Half-hardy annual	4	Stems need wiring. Dry face down
Pink (*Dianthus*)	Hardy perennial	2	Retains colour very well
Pansy (*Viola wittrockiana*)	Hardy perennial	2–3	Stems need wiring
Polyanthus (*Primula*)	Hardy perennial	2	Push wire into calyx to prevent flower heads falling off
Rose		2–3	Small buds give best results
Stock		2–3	Double flowers are prettiest
Sweet pea (*Lathyrus*)	Hardy annual	2–3	Red colours strengthen considerably
Violet (*Viola*)	Hardy annual	1	Keeps colour well
Wallflower	Hardy biennial	2	Sprays may be lain flat
Zinnia	Half-hardy annual	2–3	Dry face down. Small varieties dry most successfully

Chapter 3

How to Press Flowers and Leaves

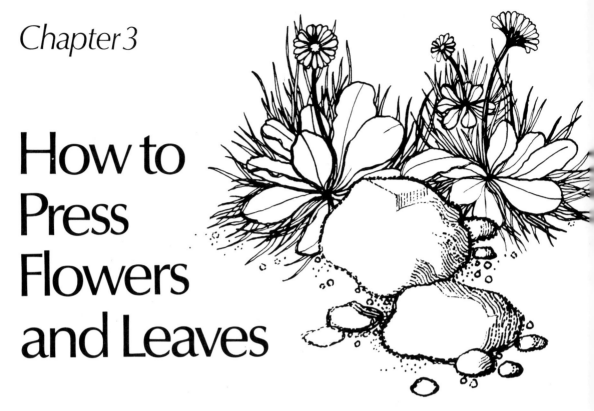

At a very early age, children discover that they can make their precious bunches of wild or garden flowers last indefinitely by pressing them carefully between sheets of newspaper. Unfortunately, however, since patience is not usually one of the virtues endowed on the young, it is only if they forget entirely about the project that the flowers and leaves have the chance to dry successfully. But basically the process is as simple as that. It is a matter of collecting plant material on a dry day, laying it carefully between two sheets of blotting paper (infinitely better than newspaper, which tends to shed its printing ink), weighting it down and leaving in a warm, dry place for at least four to six weeks. The flowers, leaves, stalks, grasses and ferns, once they have thoroughly dried out, can be used to make enchanting greeting cards and both abstract and life-like pictures.

It is important to press all the material, but most particularly delicate flowers that would quickly wilt, absolutely fresh. The serious collector, therefore, will take blotting paper and books or a flower press out on a country walk and press the flowers on the spot. And, indeed, on a warm sunny day, with a picnic to look forward to, there can be few more pleasant ways to spend an afternoon. There is one obvious potential hazard, though; the slightest breath of wind will play havoc with sheets of cow parsley, buttercup or daisy flowers. Otherwise take a jar of water and stand the flowers in it as you pick them.

The list of suitable material which follows includes the material used in our designs but is by no means complete; experiment by pressing a page of any you like—as long as they are not too bumpy. Flowers with thick centres or very fleshy leaves are not suitable; the absorbent paper would not be able to come into contact with the shallower surfaces.

All is not lost, however, if you do want to press flowers which have thick centres. It just takes longer, because you have to pull off each individual petal, press them singly so that no two are touching on the page, and reassemble them again for a life-like effect. Trumpet-shaped flowers, such as bluebells, can be sliced in half—two for the price of one—and then pressed.

You can buy simple flower presses, often in toy shops, since the hobby is so popular with children, or you can make one from several sheets of chipboard or other board that will not readily warp, and thumb-screws. Diagram 2 shows the materials you will need to make one—two 12-inch squares of plywood, with a hole drilled 1-inch in from each corner; 12-inch squares of corrugated cardboard and of blotting paper, both with corners cut off. To make a press as shown in Diagram 3, use six sheets of cardboard and ten squares of blotting paper. Fasten the press with a screw and wing nut at each corner. Place the materials in this order: plywood, cardboard, two sheets of blotting paper, cardboard and so on. The time-honoured method, however, is still perfectly satisfactory: sheets of blotting paper interleaved between the pages of a large book, as we show in the colour photograph on page 10. Any heavy book that you can spare for a few weeks will do; though be sure to choose one that you will not constantly want to refer to, such as a cookery book, and if possible use one with matt and not shiny pages.

Press only one kind of plant material on each layer or page. Arrange it carefully so that no single leaf or flower touches another one. You will find that this part of the exercise becomes as fascinating as a jig-saw puzzle, twisting and turning the material so that you can fit in as many shapes as possible on the space.

Use a pair of fine tweezers to move the material, pushing one blade well under the flower or leaf

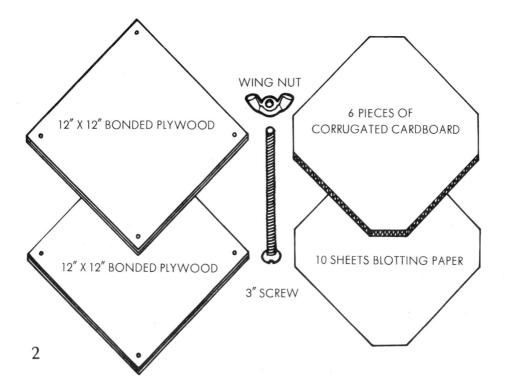

WING NUT

12" X 12" BONDED PLYWOOD

6 PIECES OF
CORRUGATED CARDBOARD

12" X 12" BONDED PLYWOOD

10 SHEETS BLOTTING PAPER

3" SCREW

2

so that you grasp it firmly in the centre. Dragging it along by the edge is likely to cause damage. Persuade stalks of buttercup, primrose, clematis montana and so on to bend into gentle curving shapes that will add movement and interest to your designs. Ram-rod straight lines are rarely attractive or desirable in work of this kind. Carefully cover the sheet of blotting paper with another, bringing it down slowly so that you do not create a rush of air. You do not want your carefully arranged material to be blown about at this stage! Label each section clearly before covering it with another layer of the press or folding the book.

Do not disturb the material for at least four weeks, though in the case of very fleshy flowers or leaves, you may look to see whether the blotting paper has become saturated. If it has, replace the top layer with a fresh one. The drying process continues for up to a year and the longer material is left the thinner it will become. Longer pressing has one great benefit: it makes the stronger-coloured flowers and petals more resistant to fading when they are brought out into the light. A word on fading: blue and violet colours are not always satisfactorily retained, particularly when

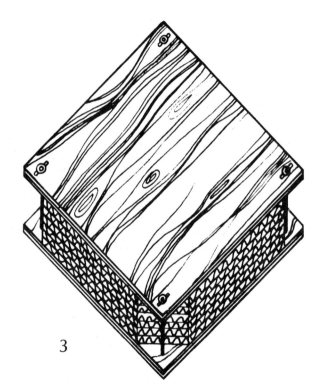

3

they have been pressed for only the minimum length of time, and often fade to a deep cream colour after several weeks. It is well to bear this in mind when designing a picture and not to feel too disappointed or cheated if it does happen.

Pressed material will reabsorb moisture if it is stored in a damp atmosphere, and could then develop mildew. To save sorting through when you are ready to work on a picture, it is a good idea to store each type of flower, leaf and stalk in a separate transparent envelope. You can buy these in photographic shops; or make them with sheets of transparent or tracing paper. Diagram 4 shows an

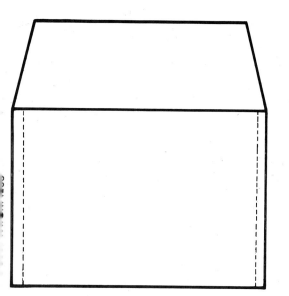

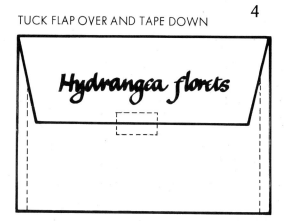

Hydrangea florets

envelope made from a twice-folded sheet of paper, strengthened with one layer of blotting paper inside and sealed with transparent adhesive tape. Store about a dozen of these envelopes underneath a book. When you are ready to use them, it will be easy to flip through the see-through covers to find just the material you want.

Suitable materials for pressing

Berberis	Press the leaves singly
Blackberry (*Rubus*)	Press leaves singly or in sprays of three
Broom (*Cytisus*)	Press flower sprays
Buttercup (*Ranunculus*)	To press stalks, bend them between thumb and first finger to give "movement" to the shape. Press flowers separately
Camomile (*Anthemis*)	Flowers fade to a soft cream when pressed; press stalks separately
Campanula	Snip out centres before pressing
Clover	Separate the leaves to emphasise the trefoil. Persuade stalks into curving shapes. Flowers can be pressed on stalks or separately
Clematis	All varieties, including the wild ones, are suitable. Press flowers, leaves and stalks all separately

Cow Parsley	Press down well in the centre to flatten. When dried, they are like exquisite snowflakes. Dry a selection of all sizes. Treat these delicate flowers with extreme care
Daffodil	One fresh flower equals two pressed ones. Separate the petals, cut the trumpet in half before treating. Reassemble in pictures
Daisy (*Bellis*)	Very thick-centred flowers are not suitable. All others respond well. Pink daisies turn mauve in drying
Dogwood (*Cornus*)	The leaves are variegated green and cream
Fennel (*Foeniculum*)	The frondy leaves are very tender to handle
Ferns	All kinds are good subjects for pressing. Very large leaves can be snipped into more manageable sprays
Globe Thistle (*Echinops*)	The dramatic outline of the leaves is invaluable in a collection
Grasses	All types of grass, except thick, stubby heads, press well, and are very versatile in pressed flower pictures and other designs
Hellebore (*Helleborus corsicus*)	The long, thin leaves have pronounced veins when dried
Honeysuckle (*Lonicera*)	Press leaves and flowers separately
Hydrangea	The florets fade to soft colours, green, pink or blue
Ivy (*Hedera*)	Press leaves of all sizes, from the smallest you can find
Lamb's Ear (*Stachys*)	Press the white woolly leaves
Maidenhair Fern (*Adiantum*)	Light as a feather, these leaves can only be handled on very still days
Malus	Trees are so tall, one usually has to be content with washing and drying fallen leaves
Michaelmas Daisy (*Aster*)	Press flowers. Need heavy weight to flatten centre
Marigold (*Calendula*)	Snip out some centres before pressing—they are useful by themselves—and press some petals individually

Narcissus	Dismantle flowers, press parts separately and re-assemble for pictures
Nipplewort (*Lapsana*)	Press the flowers
Oak (*Quercus*)	Press leaves
Pansy (*Viola*)	Press petals separately. The deep blue flowers will unfortunately fade to cream after exposure to strong light
Pelargonium	Press leaves
Primrose (*Primula*)	Press stalks and flowers separately
Raspberry (*Rubus*)	Pick some leaves which are red-and-green coloured, and silver-backed, in a range of sizes
Rock Geranium	Press leaves
Rose	Press petals separately. White ones will "fade" to cream; red ones turn brown
Rowan or Mountain Ash (*Sorbus*)	Press the leaves; they give far more pleasing results than when they are preserved with the berries
Santolina or Lavender Cotton	Small sprigs dry well; the little feather shapes could be used to represent trees in pictures
Senecio (*Ligularia*)	A useful two-toned material in silver/green
Smoke Tree or Sumach (*Rhus*)	Pick at intervals to collect the leaves in a range of colours
Thyme, Wild	Strip off lower leaves and press short sprays
Tulip (*Tulipa*)	Press velvety petals singly
Vetch (*Vicia*)	Press the violet-blue flowers
Violet (*Viola*)	Press the flowers
Virginia Creeper (*Vitis*)	Pick leaves of all sizes. They give warm, glowing red tones
Yarrow (*Achillea Millefolium*)	Very good for large picture designs. Press the umbrella-shaped heads and the leaves separately

Ironing

Some leaves can be pressed with a warm iron. The process does not give quite the long-lasting results achieved by the more conventional method, but then it takes only a few minutes instead of several weeks. Place the leaves between two sheets of blotting paper or newspaper and press with a warm iron until the plant material has dried out–about five minutes.

Grasses, pampas, montbretia and gladioli leaves respond to this treatment; which is just as well, because the elongated spiky leaves are obstinately longer than most flower presses and books used for the purpose. The leaves of fatsia japonica, smoke tree or sumach (*Rhus*), horse chestnut (*Aesculus*) and beech can be ironed in this way, too.

Skeletonising

You can often find skeletonised leaves in the garden, perhaps underneath a holly tree; the perfect, finely veined structure on which the plant tissue was built. Skeletonised magnolia leaves, sometimes bleached and sometimes dyed, can be bought in florists' shops and through flower clubs; they give interesting textural contrast in so many natural plant designs.

Collect undamaged leaves of ivy, laurel, magnolia, avocado and holly. Boil half a regular-sized box of blue household detergent powder in a large saucepan of water. Add the leaves and boil for 30 minutes. Remove and hold under cold running water. Use an old toothbrush or something similar and brush each leaf to remove the green plant tissue. Blot the leaves between sheets of newspaper or blotting paper to dry and then iron to flatten them. Do not iron holly; it has too much natural curve and will break.

Chapter 4

How to Preserve Leaves and Berries

Preserving leaves and berries in a glycerine or other solution gives them a permanent glow, as if they have been polished by the setting sun. It has a roaring-log-fire on a cold winter's day kind of effect, the leaves shining like copper round the hearth, the berries and fruits glinting among them like sparks.

If you have ever admired a walk of trees or hedging shrubs when the leaves are falling, and wished you could capture that moment for ever, this is the way to do it—though you have to gather your material one season earlier, while the plant is still absorbing moisture, and before it begins to dry out. With the exception of house plants and evergreens, plant material should be gathered in midsummer.

The preparation can be done in next to no time, about as long as it takes to boil an egg, though after that the waiting time, while the solution does its work, varies from a few days to thirteen weeks. Meanwhile, however, you have a colourful, interesting and constantly changing display, as the colour photograph on page 11 shows; a whole collection of material at different stages of preservation clustered round an old elm kneading trough in a morning room.

Material preserved in this way emerges soft and supple, and without the brittleness characteristic of the drying process described in Chapter 2. The principle is this: the stems, sprays or individual leaves take up the moisture, a mixture of glycerine or other compound, which is carried to every part of the plant material—leaves, buds, berries. As the water evaporates the glycerine is retained by the plant cells and preserves the material in its entirety.

Almost all preserved leaves change colour; they will turn deep russet brown, as beech does, black, like laurel, dark green, steel blue or reddish brown. To lighten them again stand them on a sunny windowsill for a week or two after preservation.

Rose hips and red berries will fade slightly to deep orange; and yellow berries deepen to golden orange. Blackberry fruits, one of the most exciting materials to preserve, shrink a little but retain the denseness of their colour.

To prepare the plant material remove all damaged or blemished leaves, scrape off bark and split the ends of woody stems for about 2 inches.

There are two recipes for plant-preserving solution, one using glycerine and the other motor car anti-freeze liquid. Although glycerine is by far the more expensive, the unabsorbed solution can be stored in a covered jar, reheated and used over and over again, so the outlay is not a continuing one.

5

First, glycerine: use one part glycerine to two parts very hot water. Pour the liquids into a bottle, cork tightly and shake well until the solution is thoroughly mixed. If you do not do this, the glycerine will sink to the bottom and the plant material will take up the liquids unevenly. To increase absorption rate in thick, woody stems, bring the solution to boiling point and use immediately. The alternative is to mix motor car anti-freeze liquid with an equal quantity of hot water; shake or stir until thoroughly blended. Again, the solution can be boiled for use with hard, woody stems. The mixtures are interchangeable and equally successful, but give slightly different colours to the

40

preserved material. Whichever solution is used, pour it into a container in scale with the plant material, so that the solution will reach about 2 inches up the stems (Diagram 5). For large sprays of leaves, such as oak and beech, you can use an earthenware jug, catering-size coffee tin or stone jar. Naturally, when boiling solution is used, you must not pour it into glass vessels. For single leaves, small sprays of sycamore or maple keys and materials on this scale, use jam jars, old cups or mugs. Watch to see that the plant material does not absorb all the solution before preservation is complete. If it does, pour in more hot-water solution (not boiling this time) to restore the original level. Beads of moisture appearing on the surface of the leaves are an indication that the material has already been in the substance too long and cannot absorb any more. Remove it and gently pat off the moisture, using a soft cloth or tissues.

Conversely, if the tips of some leaves begin to dry out and become brittle it means that the stems are absorbing the solution too slowly; the situation can be rectified by rubbing the leaves on both sides with cotton wool soaked in the preserving solution. This trouble is frequently encountered with heavy-tissue leaves such as fatsia japonica, fig and ivy; it can be avoided by totally immersing the leaves in hot (not boiling) solution instead of standing them in a partly filled container.

When the leaf colour has changed and there is no sign or sound of brittleness, the material can be said to be preserved. The time varies considerably according to the thickness of the plant tissue, from less than a week in the case of beech leaves to one month for laurel and camellia leaves and three months for aspidistra leaves.

Once material has been preserved, you can safely use it with fresh flowers for it will not take up any more water. Store in a cool, dry room to retain its suppleness.

Suitable material for preserving

Material	Approximate number of weeks to preserve	Notes
Aspidistra	2–3 weeks immersed 13 weeks upright	Immersion gives better results
Bay (Laurus nobilis)	2	Leaves deepen to dark olive green
Beech (Fagus)	½–1	Cut when fully mature but before drying. Treat in large sprays
Bells of Ireland (Molucella)	3	Preserve then hang upside down to dry. Bracts become papery
Berberis	3	Treat long stems. Leaves turn deep brown

Material	Approximate number of weeks to preserve	Notes
Blackberry (*Rubus Fruticosus*)	3	Treat sprays of leaves and berries
Cotoneaster	3–5	Treat leaves and buds. Leaves turn leather brown, silver on reverse
Cypress (*Cupressus Lawsoniana*)	3–4	Treat flat fan-shaped sprays complete with "cones"
Dock	2	Cut small spikes of seedheads. The red colour deepens most effectively
Escallonia	2	The long straight sprays of minute leaves are ideal for outlining shape
Fatsia japonica	2–3 weeks immersed 10 weeks upright	The evergreen foliage turns mid brown in glycerine, dark brown in anti-freeze
Fig	1–2 weeks immersed 6–7 weeks upright	Treat leaves singly
Gum tree (*Eucalyptus*)	2–3	Leaves turn pale grey-mauve
Hellebore (*Helleborus corsicus*)	3	Leaves turn light brown in glycerine, darker in anti-freeze
Holly (*Ilex*)	3	Treat leaves and berries together. Spray berries after preservation with ordinary hair lacquer
Ivy (*Hedera*)	$1\frac{1}{2}$–2 weeks immersed 3 weeks or more upright, depending on length of material	Long sprays are best immersed. Berries can be treated, too
Laurel (*Laurus nobilis*)	4	Anti-freeze better than glycerine. Leaves turn almost black

Material	Approximate number of weeks to preserve	Notes
Mahonia	3–6	Leaves darken progressively. Take out after 3 weeks if light colour preferred. Sometimes 2-tone effect achieved
Maidenhair fern (*Adiantum*)	2	Cut at any time as it is evergreen
Maple (*Acer*)	2	Treat single leaves, and clusters of keys. Sprays of different varieties give wide colour range from light to very dark
Mistletoe	2	Treat small sprays with berries. They wither in time
Oak (*Quercus*)	2–3	Oak apples and acorns preserve well on the stems
Old Man's Beard (*Clematis vitalba*)	2	Gather before flowers open. If this is not possible spray with hair lacquer after treatment
Peony (*Paeonia*)	2	Leaves turn pale olive green with dark contrasting veins
Pyracantha	3	All varieties, with red, yellow or orange berries, preserve well. Spray berries after treatment with hair lacquer to prevent or delay shrivelling
Raspberry (*Rubus*)	2	Cut young, perfect leaves. They turn dark red with silver underneath
Rhododendron	3	Preserve sprays of leaves with young, tight buds
Rose briars	2	Young shoots of wild roses preserve well. Use solution at boiling point
Rose hips	2–3	Spray hips with hair lacquer after preserving

Material	Approximate number of weeks to preserve	Notes
Rosemary (*Rosmarinus officinalis*)	2	Stems after preserving are silver grey. Scent is retained in leaves
Rowan or Mountain Ash (*Sorbus*)	2–3	Sprays of leaves and berries are a dramatic combination of nut brown and orange. Lacquer-spray berries
Shoo-fly Plant (*Nicandra*)	2	Treat in solution then hang upside down to dry
Silver Birch (*Betula*)	4	Cut with catkins on twigs. Colour shades from yellow to deep brown. Use solution at boiling point
Snakeweed (*Polygonum*)	2–3	Fine sprays of dark red flowers keep colour well
Snowberry (*Symphoricarpos*)	2–3	Sprays of the white or pinky-white snowberries deepen in colour in the process
Sweet Chestnut (*Castanea sativa*)	$1\frac{1}{2}$–2	Preserve in three stages—with tiny chestnuts; later, still with catkins; and more without catkins. Catkins stiffen into interesting shapes
Sycamore (*Platanus*)	1–$1\frac{1}{2}$	Treat leaves and keys
Viburnum	3	Leaves turn deep brown with olive brown on reverse
White Cedar (*Chamaecyparis*)	3	Leaves turn marmalade colour. Do not remove from solution when they are just brown
Yew (*Taxus*)		Berries do not always preserve well but it is worth trying. Leaves can be cut at any time

46

Chapter 5

Cards for all Occasions

Even a young child can design a greeting card; indeed, some of the most endearing messages we will ever receive are those lovingly made for us as part of a school project, or simply as an expression of thoughtfulness.

And, since it is the thought that counts, making greeting cards is a good way to start using your pressed flowers and leaves. Cards are on a reassuringly small scale; they do not take very long to work and quickly give the satisfaction of achievement. Added to that, they represent little if any outlay on materials, and next to nothing is lost if your first experiments are not entirely to your liking. If a special birthday, or Christmas, isn't just around the corner, then invent a reason for sending a card. Anyone would appreciate one expressing congratulations on an examination success; good wishes at the start of a new job or as a token saying Get Well Soon.

The four greeting cards shown in the colour photograph on page 12 are each pressed flower pictures in miniature. The greeting is put in with "instant" lettering, the kind you can buy in artists' material shops, in large sheets to transfer on to your page.

Each of the four cards is worked on a sheet of cartridge paper $4\frac{1}{2}$ by 9 inches (11·5 by 23 cm), folded in two to give a $4\frac{1}{2}$-inch (11·5 cm) square. The corners are slightly rounded, by drawing round a coin before cutting.

Once they are dry, pressed flowers and leaves are brittle and need handling with the utmost care; a pair of tweezers will be helpful. Transparent rubber solution (Cow gum) is one of the most suitable adhesives to use. If necessary, you can move the plant material about a little after placing, and then tidy up any remaining traces of the solution with a small ball formed of the dried-up rubber.

It is important to use the solution sparingly; take it from a tube (or tin) on the point of a spent matchstick, cocktail or orange stick.

To Rose

First, almost a poem in itself, the card "To Rose". With a name like that, the design is almost a foregone conclusion—one perfect rose.

With such simplicity, the success of the design depends on care and neatness. The flower is formed of five white rose petals, "faded" to a pale parchment cream after pressing. Look through your page of pressed petals and select five perfectly matched in both size and colour. Choose two pressed stalks of clematis montana with gently flowing natural curves to give "movement" to your design.

Place the stalks and rose petals on the face of your card, or on a sheet of white paper cut to the same size; build up the design completely before applying the adhesive so that you can correct any imperfections or alter the scale or balance of the material.

For the flower centre, use a mauve clover flower, and for the sepals, two tiny clematis montana leaves, well matched for size. You will need five leaves to form the spray and one single leaf on the other side of the stalk. Use rose leaves, if you have them, or any others with serrated edges. We used ash leaves.

Before sticking down the plant material, very lightly pencil in guide lines for the lettering. If you are using instant lettering from a sheet, line up each letter in turn; press on top of it with the rounded end of a paintbrush handle or the cap of a ball-point pen. As each letter is transferred on to the card, cover it with a small piece of thin paper and rub it over again to press it well into the paper. Take great care to allow equal spacing between each letter and the next, so that your card has the look of craftsman printing.

Using the rubber solution very sparingly, stick down the stalks, petals, flower and leaves. Place a sheet of fine paper, such as tracing paper, over the design and very gently press down each piece.

Best Wishes

With just "Best Wishes" on the face of the card, it is up to you to spell out your message inside: you can send this card on all the "unbirthday" occasions you want to mark.

The two flowers are campanula with centres snipped out so that the flowers lie flat for pressing. In the design these centres have been replaced by daisies, face down on the card. The stems are buttercup stalks and the leaves snippets of maidenhair fern. At the base there is another daisy—placed right way up this time—and four honeysuckle leaves complete the design.

Birthday Greetings

The sunniest birthday greeting imaginable, a design in shiny buttercup yellow. Pressed buttercup flowers and buds are used with buttercup stalks, the only "outsiders" being the small rock geranium leaves.

It may be a little difficult at first to achieve a pleasing balance between the plant material and the message, since the words are both comparatively long ones. To prevent the buttercup spray looking pushed to one side of the card, trace out the letters from the sheet first, work out the spacing evenly, and then design the spray around them. A graceful, flowing curve extending above the message will help the balance immeasurably.

Valentine's Day

There's a wealth of sentiment in a hand-made Valentine card. This one could become a treasured heirloom, like the nineteenth-century ones which are popular with collectors today.

Camomile flowers and buds are the main feature of the design, with buttercup stalks and tiny pieces of santolina. The five large leaves are raspberry, a rich, deep red. For the very small leaves, you can use any well-shaped, rounded leaves from your collection – berberis, for example.

Music Cards

It's a romantic and pretty idea, anyway, to make a card for someone special, so we have carried the sentiment one stage further and designed two cards with nosegays of pressed flowers adorning snippets of sheet music. These happen to be earnest love songs, but you can adapt the idea in a number of ways, pasting on to a lyric or a snatch of music that holds very special memories for just two people, a cutting from a theatre programme or a wedding invitation, anything that is both decorative and meaningful.

"The Dear Little Thing"

The card with the sand-coloured background (you can see them in colour on page 13) is a tribute to "The Dear Little Thing", a song published with the music for *The Casino Girl*, a musical which played at The Shaftesbury Theatre in London and The Casino, New York. The words are by Raymond St. Leonards and the music by Alfred Delbruck. The first verse sets the theme for the flower border. It must be as dainty and pretty as the song:

> "Her eyes were the bluest of blue,
> Her heart was so loving and true:
> A dear little thing,
> As dainty as Spring,
> And fresh as the sweet morning dew."

From our pressed flower collection we chose pale lavender-coloured hydrangea florets, daisies, clover flowers, camomile buds and stalks and cow parsley. For the leaves, rock geranium, raspberry, minute petals of broom, small red berberis leaves and snatches of an on-the-spot pressing expedition across marshland.

A rock geranium leaf is centred above the music, covered with an hydrangea floret and surrounded by a fan of "half" daisies pressed on their stalks. The motif is repeated below the music, with another rock geranium leaf and hydrangea floret, more half daisies, two clover flowers and now a circle of cow parsley centred by a full daisy flower, face downwards. The corners of the music are covered by two daisies and two clover flowers with small leaves, petals and snippings of cow parsley scattered in a wind-blown way—but always symmetrical.

To make the card, we used a piece of stiff white card $13\frac{1}{2}$ by $9\frac{5}{8}$ inches (34 by 25 cm) which, doubled, gives a finished area of $6\frac{3}{4}$ by $9\frac{5}{8}$ inches (17 by 25 cm). Make it much smaller than this and it will be difficult to decorate with a good balance of flowers—enough to be colourful and interesting, yet not so many that it looks crowded.

The background is a piece of sand-coloured, textured card, the corners cut round a coin. Stick the background on to the card and the piece of sheet music in position before commencing the design. Measure carefully from top to bottom and from side to side to make sure that everything is correctly positioned.

As always, sort through your collection and match pairs of leaves and flowers for both colour and size, then try out the design by putting everything in place before applying the adhesive. Use rubber solution sparingly, on the end of a small piece of stick.

To finish the card, tie a neat bow with $\frac{1}{4}$-inch (7 mm) wide baby ribbon, secure the knot with a few stitches and stick it in the centre of the left-hand edge. Protect the card with an inner Cellophane paper envelope before sending it in the post.

"If Love Were All"

The second card is worked on a Valentine's Day pink cotton background, the song an example of the sweetly sentimental mood of the period. Words are by Edward Teschemacher, music by Landon Ronald:

"If love were all, I'd pluck the fairest flow'r
 That in life's garden grows at summer's hour,
 And give it to thee with a dewy pall,
 If love were all."

The natural materials include santolina buds and frondy leaves, hydrangea florets, sprays of wild thyme, the pressed centres of two roses, nipplewort flowers and senecio leaves.

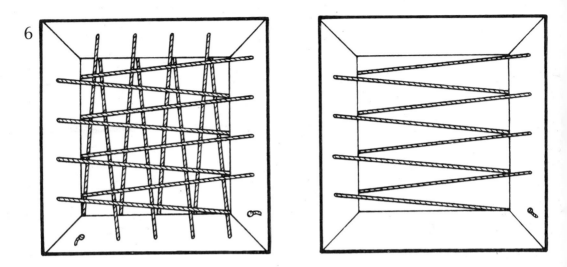

Above the music, a corn-coloured hydrangea floret and a rose centre are cupped by four sprays of wild thyme. Below the music, two senecio leaves make a dark background for a pale lavender-coloured hydrangea floret, another rose centre and fronds of santolina. A single spray of off-white santolina buds hangs from this motif like a peal of bells.

The finished doubled size of the white card is $6\frac{3}{4}$ inches (17 cm) wide by $7\frac{1}{2}$ inches (19 cm) high. For the background, cut a piece of cotton approximately this size. Cut a piece of card slightly smaller and lay it in the centre of the cotton, wrong side of fabric uppermost. Turn the fabric overlap over the card on all four sides. Secure it on the back with stitches taken from top to bottom, then from side to side, pulling the material tight so that it leaves no wrinkles on the face of the card (Diagram 6). Stick this fabric-covered card to the white card before commencing the flower design.

Finish the card with a bow of white $\frac{1}{4}$-inch (7 mm) wide ribbon.

Chapter 6

'Painting' with Pressed Flowers

If you have already made some greeting cards and other small mementoes for your friends, and have got the feel of working with pressed flowers, it is now time to design a picture—probably the aim of everyone who has built up a sizeable collection of pressed material.

Although design is a very personal thing, there are certain guidelines which it is helpful to follow. However, before beginning to put, as it were, pen to paper, there are a few rules, or rather elements, which must be carefully noted.

They largely have to do with the conditions under which you store and handle the pressed material. It has already been mentioned that these delicate items are subject to reabsorption of moisture and must never at any time be exposed to dampness. This means that your flowers, leaves, grasses and stalks must be kept in a warm, dry, airy room, and preferably in envelopes or packets of some kind until you are ready to start work.

Once you start, the same conditions must apply. And if it is a windy day, or you live in a house noted for its draughtiness, be sure to work out of range of any strong current of air. It is far from amusing to find that a carefully laid scheme is wafted away on a gentle breeze.

It does not really matter whether you fit your pressed flower picture to an existing frame or have one made to fit round it; there is a slight advantage to having the frame made first, because then you will have the glass exactly the size of your picture background, and can place it over blotting paper on top of your work each time you have to be interrupted.

The best material to use as a background is artists' mounting board, which you can buy in a range of colours from white and cream to darker shades. As covering board satisfactorily with coloured paper is a difficult task—without proper heat-bonding, wrinkles in the surface are almost inevitable—try to find a colour of the board which suits your purpose. Have the board professionally cut to the exact size of the frame, if you have it. When the picture is completed have it backed with a piece of hardboard. It is essential to achieve a really tight fit within the depth of the frame so that the picture is pushed against the glass. For this reason, you must on no account have a mount made to surround your picture; it would create a cavity between the natural materials and the glass and cause deterioration.

When the time comes to take your picture to be framed, cover it with blotting paper, with a piece of glass if you have it or with a stiff, warp-resistant board if not, and seal round the edges with adhesive tape. Wait until the framer is ready to start work on it before you take it, in case the workshop is damp.

It is a fact of life, that many of your dried-by-pressing materials will eventually fade in the light; some more quickly than others. To give them the best chance of colour retention, always hang a pressed flower picture on a north wall, away from direct sunlight. It is not going too far to put it away in a cupboard or wrapped in brown paper in the height of the summer if you are lucky enough to live in a district where excessive sunlight is a problem.

Yellow and orange colours have been found to have the best record of colour retention and of these the yellow daisy, anthemis, is best of all. Celandine, for example, fades to cream or white in about a year; most other yellows will keep their identity for up to three years, but anthemis can be still going strong, as bright as ever, after about ten years.

Among the blue colours, delphinium and larkspur flowers are far and away the most satisfying from this point of view. If you plan a design in which blue is important, it is advisable to use one or other of these two flowers. Others that you might choose, such as campanulas, cornflowers, violets, forget-me-nots and pansies, will all gradually soften to varying shades of cream.

Rose petals, too, have a mind of their own and all the pale colours, including white, will turn cream; all the dark ones, including deep red, will turn brown.

This colour change, sometimes gradual and sometimes almost before your eyes, is one of the fascinating things about the hobby. It is almost as if the material lives on and continues to develop and all that you have captured is a shape, a form and a texture.

For this reason, shape and balance are vital in every design. The designer has a responsibility to see to it that every single flower and leaf is shown to its best advantage and that the materials do not crowd each other or vie for the viewer's attention.

The most restful and graceful pictures are those where the design radiates from an important central feature, often the largest flower or group of flowers, as in the picture shown in colour on page 14, or takes a gentle, sweeping arc or curve. It is only a very skilled designer who can make a completely at-random design come together attractively.

It is impossible to over-emphasise the importance of leaves and stalks in a collection of pressed materials. Some designers find that, without even thinking about it, they tend to use leaves and flowers in the proportion of two to one. And for those who are unfamiliar with the art, this is quite a good plan. As leaves will change colour less than many flowers, allowance does not have to be made at the design stage for the colour they are likely to be in a year's time.

Stalks can take the place of drawn or painted lines in a picture; they give shape and movement;

64

can be used to carry the eye to and from a focal point and, besides that, provide something almost literally to "hang things on": sprays of nearly-natural-looking flowers can be made up with separate petals ranged on both sides of a curving stalk. You will have induced curves into the stalks as you pressed them; if you have to join two or three lengths, conceal the joins with a carefully placed flower, leaf or petal that just happens to do two jobs at once.

When you are beginning pressed flower picture design, you might well find that your enthusiasm to make a start has preceded your ability to build up a large and varied collection of material. But you will soon find that by taking a little artist's licence you can enormously increase the versatility of what you have.

With a small, sharp pair of manicure scissors you can snip a large leaf into a smaller one, exactly the shape you want, even serrate a leaf if you have the skill and patience; with a small pot of white poster paint you can add highlights to a cream flower or petal – cow parsley, for instance. A few minute dabs of white paint will make the delicate flower heads more like snowflakes than ever. And by superimposing a flower on a leaf, one flower on another, the decorative and pretty middle of one on to the less attractive centre of another; a light petal on a dark leaf or vice versa, you will soon find that your collection, however small, has endless possibilities.

Look through your material and try to form an overall impression of what you have; get an idea of the type of effect you want to create, and the general colour scheme. Perhaps one particular flower or leaf might suggest an idea. For example, the picture on page 66 of an elderly couple going to the opera, was suggested by nothing more tangible than a pair of small clematis montana leaves which looked like a moustache!

If you have amassed predominantly dark leaves, such as ash, clematis montana, honeysuckle and poplar, which are black; dark brown leaves like oak, and deep crimson ones like cherry and blackberry, there is a good case for choosing a pale coloured background against which they will be strongly silhouetted. Do not choose white, though; the complete contrast would probably be too much.

On the other hand, if you have been pressing material from a corner of the garden where silver-leafed plants abound, such as lamb's ear, senecio, sea holly, cineraria and centaurea, then you might well decide that nothing but a black background could show them to the full.

Picture in graded circles
We chose a black background for the picture on page 14, and worked a symmetrical design in ever-increasing circles radiating from a central group of cow parsley flower heads. Although the colour scheme includes the mid-pink of the hydrangea florets and daisies, the mauve of the Michaelmas daisies, the variegated yellow and green of the cornus leaves and the two-tone red and green of both the pelargonium and raspberry leaves, it is the silver that predominates; the wheel-like pattern created by the lamb's ear leaves has pride of place.

We give general instructions for building up a concentric design of this type, though you will obviously adapt them to suit the materials you have. The first important thing is to sort through your materials and pick out the leaves and flower heads you need which match for size. Notice that the wheel of variegated cornus uses three sizes of the leaves – four large ones, four medium sized and eight smaller ones – all matched pairs. These leaves were pressed by ironing. Discard any material that has become damaged, either during or since pressing, unless it is vital to your design and you can disguise the fault by placing something on top of it.

Use the adhesive very sparingly, preferably on the point of a sharpened matchstick or cocktail stick. Apply the tiniest dab in the centre of daisy-type flowers; at the tip and at intervals along alternate sides of sprays of flowers; at intervals along the spine of large leaves and in small dabs along the lengths of stalk. There is no need to apply adhesive to the tips of petals when the whole flower is used; the centre is quite enough. Remember that the picture will be pressed against the glass when it is framed.

This design was, of course, started in the centre, with a ring of cow parsley. Then the wheel of cornus leaves, carefully alternated for size and, at the tips of each of the smallest ones, a Michaelmas daisy, pressed so that it is folded over and looks like half a flower, and a minute leaf of broom. When the adhesive has set on the cow parsley and cornus leaves you can place four more overlapping circles of cow parsley and a Michaelmas daisy, pressed out flat this time, right in the centre.

Next comes a ring of lawn daisies, some right way up and some upside down, the bright green calyces as attractive as the yellow centres of the neighbouring flowers.

After that, the lamb's ear leaves, two pairs at the top and two at the bottom. Notice how well these leaves combine with the small clippings of mugwort used in the same layer.

These leaves, found growing wild on wasteground, are deep, bright green on one side and silvery grey on the other.

Also in this row, there are four small red and green pelargonium leaves and two three-leaved sprays of raspberry, in the same colours. These leaves, of course, are reversible and equally attractive used with the silver underside uppermost. In the next ring, larger pelargonium leaves are alternated with sprigs of wild thyme, the pink flowers almost exactly matching the outer ring of deep pink hydrangea florets.

Unless a design is made for a round frame, when a completely circular pattern is acceptable, it is usually more effective to add an extra motif either at the top or bottom of the circle, as a final flourish, so to speak. In this case, the finishing touch is a fan-like motif at the top. First, there are two sprays of rowan leaves, used to show the strong lines of the veining on the undersides. In the centre, a large pink daisy acts as the radius for sprays of couch grass, the stems gently persuaded, before pressing, into graceful curves. These sprays are embellished with tiny sprigs of the semi-formed buds of hydrangea and, at the top, a crescent of tiny cornus leaves.

Opera-goers
This is the picture which was suggested by a pair of clematis montana leaves. It is worked on a piece of cream mounting board and displayed in a silver art nouveau frame.

In fact, clematis montana has a strong hand in the design. The stalks form the man's top hat, his nose, the lady's eyeglass and eyebrows; the leaves represent the man's eyebrows and moustache.

Tiny sprigs of yarrow represent his hair and her eyelashes, with camomile flowers for his eyes. His bow tie is two leaves and the stalk of a three-leafed clover and his coat, two dark red leaves and a piece of fern.

The lady's lips are a pair of tiny berberis leaves, bright red of course; the same leaves, but used the other side up, when they are pinky-beige, represent her hair. The extravagant fur-like texture of her stole? Four clover flowers.

If you can once visualise the representational possibilities in a flower or a leaf, you will find that designs of this kind are very simple to build. Perhaps a petal might suggest the arched back of a cat, or a leaf a tiny forest of Christmas trees; then the hunt is on to try and carry out your preliminary idea with the materials you have. If you are prepared to be imaginative and flexible, it is a hunt which will give you endless pleasure.

Chapter 7

Pictures
in Depth

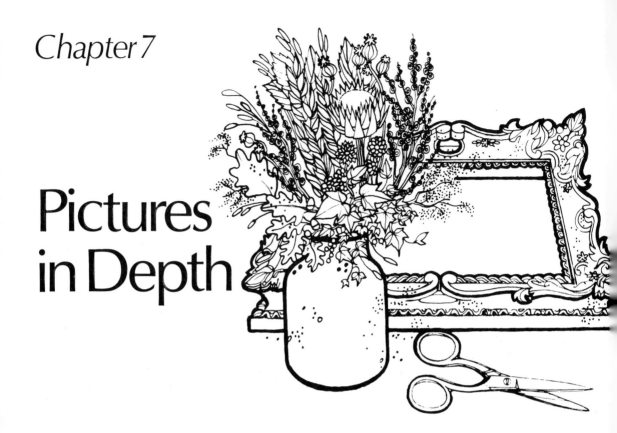

One of the loveliest ways of using dried and preserved natural materials is to compose them into a three-dimensional picture. You can make a design in any size and in any mood. It can be realistic as a posy of summer flowers, as in the colour photograph on page 15, or an abstract design where the natural materials are used just for their shape, as if they were buttons or beads. An example of this kind of treatment is shown on page 16.

The choice of frame and background are all-important and should be considered before you begin the design. Dried flower pictures, unlike pressed flower pictures, are never glazed and so if you have an old frame which has lost its glass, this would be ideal. You can try the effect of different coloured paper or fabric backgrounds behind it, spread out a selection of your dried materials and judge the colour effect as a whole. If you design the picture first, without a frame, take it with you to the framemaker's and try corner samples of the different mounts and frames round it. You will be looking for colours and textures that echo but do not overpower those in your design. Bring the picture safely away with you after the measurements have been taken; the framer might not realise just how delicate and precious it is. To be absolutely on the safe side, though it is not always possible, it is advisable to have the frame made first, right to the point of having the picture hooks and cord attached ready for hanging and to apply the design in the ready-made frame. In this way your picture will be subject to the least possible movement.

For the background, you can use self-coloured stiff card, or cover white card with closely woven fabric. To get a really wrinkle-free finish with a paper covering, the paper needs to be heat-bonded to the card—a job for professionals—whereas fabric can be pulled tight simply by sewing. The method used for both the pictures we describe is exactly the same as that used to cover the music cards in Chapter 5. Only the measurements are different. For pictures, allow an overlap of the fabric of about 2 inches (5 cm) all round the card to be folded over and sewn in at the back. Diagram 6 on page 54 shows how it is done.

Any medium-weight, closely woven fabric is suitable for a picture background and on the whole a slight texture, such as you find in linen, linen-type rayon, twill or cotton piqué, is an advantage. Plain fabrics will usually give more emphasis to the flower design and are therefore easier to handle, particularly for beginners, though a carefully chosen all-over print can be charming.

The background colour can be a complete contrast to the design material or a near match. It is largely a matter of taste, though it is important to check that the background neither takes precedance over the natural material nor is so close to it in both colour and texture that the outlines are hard to define. The background of the two pictures shown in colour are in no way interchangeable though at first sight it might seem that the pink fabric would be a perfect match for the pink rhodanthe flowers in the posy design. However, the background would utterly dominate the gentle and soft design. A background like this needs a bold geometrical shape such as the one of rows of acorns which can meet it on equal terms.

Whereas pressed leaves and flowers are flat and have only a single plane, dried and preserved materials retain their original shape and form. They curve and twist and have bulk and take up space and cast shadows, and altogether present the designer with a new set of problems. These factors should be taken into account in every stage of the design and the materials used in the way they look most natural.

Study each type of leaf, flower and seedhead you intend to use and see what, in design terms, it is capable of. Try sticking some damaged examples on to a spare piece of card to check whether a leaf can be stuck at each end without cracking in the middle; if a flower can be lain on its side without folding over in half; if a seedhead will nestle tidily within the curve of a leaf, and so on. See where the material touches the card, or how one piece fits on top of another, and note the touch points. These, and only these, are the spots where you will apply the adhesive.

Always allow one piece to dry before placing another on top of it. This might involve time and patience, perhaps leaving the picture for a few minutes until the adhesive has started to harden and you can continue without disturbing the work you have already done. If a leaf seems inclined to curl up and away from the background, weight it with a coin or two until it is set in place. If you want to set a flower half on its side, at an angle of about 45 degrees, and it looks as if it will topple over as soon as you take your fingers away, prop it up with a few coins or a piece of twig until the adhesive strengthens enough to hold it. Then gently remove the props and admire the flower which looks as if it is being gently swayed downwards by the wind.

Apply adhesive very sparingly on the touch spots. To get the merest trace of the glue, "wind" some from a tube or tin round the end of a spent matchstick or cocktail stick and apply it from there. Spread the end of the stick in a quick, narrow line along a stalk, making sure that it only touches the under surface and does not extend up and over the sides. Put only the tiniest dab on the ends of petals, just a touch on the part of a flower which lies flat. The only time when you might need to use the glue more generously is at the base of stalks, for instance on fairly heavy heads of corn, and when they are to be hidden by other materials which will cover them.

Then you can use a small blob of glue secure in the knowledge that it will have a better chance of sticking but will not leave a shiny tell-tale mark on the background. For all but the lightest pieces of natural material, for which you can use rubber solution, you should use a transparent adhesive such as Evostick. Do not use one of the instant-setting contact adhesives for, however decisive you intend to be, it is probable that you will need to move a stalk or a leaf just a little and it is reassuring to be able to.

As always, experiment with your design before sticking it down. Mark out the size of the background on a spare piece of card or fabric and move your materials around until you achieve a pleasing balance. If the design is a complicated one, make a rough sketch of it and mark and number the position of each leaf and flower. Most of all, resist the temptation to go on adding another sprig or leaf here and there long after you have a satisfactory pattern.

Measure the background diagonally from corner to corner and mark the centre point. Except in the case of asymmetrical designs, work from that point outwards.

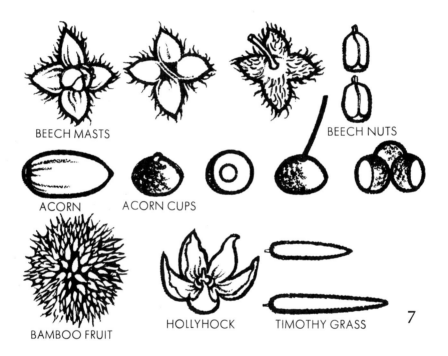

BEECH MASTS   BEECH NUTS

ACORN   ACORN CUPS

BAMBOO FRUIT   HOLLYHOCK   TIMOTHY GRASS   7

Rhodanthe posy
The frame came first and the picture followed. When we found the carved wooden frame, it was unrecognisably dirty, almost completely black. But a soft brush, barely damp, worked carefully into the crevices soon revealed the faded gilding and the traces of blue-grey surface beneath. Tougher treatment was needed on the inset, which was rubbed vigorously with sandpaper before being given a fresh coat of white paint.
The background is a Liberty cotton print combining all the surrounding colours, the gold, the steely blue and the white, but in a scale so small that it will not draw the eye away from the flower design.

The main feature of the picture is the central posy of pink and white everlasting rhodanthe flowers, some fully open and set full-face and other shyly curled buds set on their sides.

The cameo forming the base of the design, and giving a plain background on which to build, is preserved beech leaves, chosen in a range of slightly differing colours, and on top of that a ring of deep and light olive green seeds, ash "keys" used singly and in bunches, like leaves outlining a Victorian flower posy.

The dried woolly lamb's ear flowers, the papery sprays of dried sea lavender and the poppy seedheads are all greyish white, a strong contrast where they overlap the beech leaves and a softer statement where they are seen against the background fabric.

Alternating with these are the bright golden sprays of maize and the golden and brown love-in-a-mist seedheads.

Notice that all the flowers and seedheads appear to radiate from the central point, as if they are truly a posy, and only the final scattering of white rhodanthe flowers breaks away.

Acorn abstract

In a totally different mood, the geometrical design on the bright pink cotton background uses the natural materials as a series of shapes and textures, exploiting their design potential to the full. For all the variety there appears to be, the only materials used are acorns, beech mast, hollyhock seedheads, grass and bamboo fruit.

The basic idea was to work outwards from a diagonal cross which was then broken down into small lines going in different directions. To do this it is important to find and mark the centre point, draw the diagonals accurately and use a set square for the right angles made by the other lines. A studied air of casualness is what you want to achieve.

The main diagonal, from the top right to the bottom left of the picture, is made up of beech mast, the top half without any nuts and the lower ones with the nuts still in place. Note how differently the light strikes these two sections of the line and the difference it makes to the colour of the materials.

The other main diagonal, crossing this line, is made up of spiky round bamboo fruit (which we bought) at the top and individual dried hollyhock seedcases at the bottom. Beech mast features prominently again in four separate lines or blocks, now used upside down revealing the prickly uneven texture of the undersides.

Acorns lain on their sides, in rows at differing angles, like large wooden counting beads, are thick, pointed ovals and cast long, heavy shadows.

The acorn cups are used in four different ways – on their sides when they make a row of greyish brown crescents; in triple clusters like a group of bells; upside down with their stalks, rather like pom-pon hats with a tassel on the top, and upside down with their stalks broken off so that they present single domes.

Separate beech nuts are used in two separate rows, again like a bead necklace, and the sentinel-straight lines are drawn with Timothy grass heads like tiny bleached bulrushes.

Again, a clear, strong adhesive will be necessary for this design. If you encounter difficulty with any of the shiny materials, if, for instance, the acorns seem inclined to roll away after you have positioned them, you can either hold them in place for a few minutes or wedge them with a small piece of stick on either side. Diagram 7 will help you to identify the materials described.

Chapter 8

Framing with Flowers

In this age of machinery and computerised efficiency, there can be few of us who do not long just occasionally to be transported back to the days when the pace of life was kinder. To the age, for instance, when the black and white photographs on pages 25 and 26 were taken. As a tribute to times past, we selected these two scenes which so effectively capture the mood of the era, early this century, and elevate them to subjects for special treatment—framing with flowers.

We chose a harvest scene, the heat of the day, the pride of the farmhands in their labour all conveyed there in that colourless print, and decorated it with, what else, ears of corn, grasses and preserved berries the colour of poppies in the field. The mount, first a sliver of orange and then a wide band of dark sludgey green, allows all the attention to be focused on the faded print and the dried decoration.

The other photograph, of a farming family and their house nestled comfortably in a Lake District hillside, is surrounded by an even softer colour statement. It has a slip of white, then a deep cream mount, and decoration barely any stronger.

You can copy this idea with any photographs from your family album, prints found in antique shops, pencil or charcoal etchings, or photographs you can take on a country walk. How interesting it would be to surround a present-day photograph with materials you gathered on the same occasion.

Both the photographs were originally about 10 by 8 inches (25 by 20 cm); we had them profession-ally enlarged to twice that size. This process is not a cheap one, for it involves having a new negative made first. But if the print is of sentimental value, or represents a scene you enjoy recapturing,

74

it is worth the cost. Once the enlargement is mounted and framed, you have a unique picture of lasting value.

We chose to make our designs symmetrical, with the sides identical and the top and bottom motifs complementary to each other in both size and feeling. Before starting work, measure, from side to side and top to bottom, find the centre point on each edge of the mount and lightly mark it with a pencil. As always with this kind of work, select the material and try it in position first before attempting to stick anything down. It is important not to suffer a change of heart and want to move something once it is stuck; far better to perfect your design first.

Do not try to mix pressed materials with those which have been dried or preserved. Pressed leaves and flowers are flat and should be covered with glass; the others retain the natural shapes of their growing habit (and in some cases are even more curved) and should not be glazed.

When you lay each flower or leaf in place, decide how you want it to be positioned, facing outwards or on its side. Note where it touches the surface and apply the adhesive only at that spot. It is unnecessary and inappropriate to cover the entire under surface with glue. Use rubber adhesive for the lightest materials if you like, but heavier pieces such as ears of barley and anything with a spiky, uneven surface will need a heavier transparent adhesive. Weight each piece, especially the heavier ones, with a coin or something similar and leave for about five minutes until the glue has started to set.

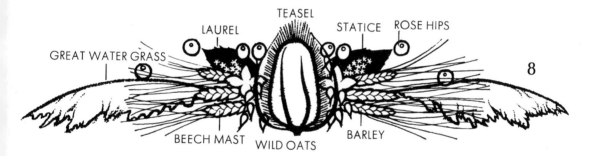

Haymaking
Think of the colours in the scene—the corn-coloured stubble, the brown earth between the rows, the red of the poppies and the white puffy clouds; these are the colours of the dried and preserved material in the decoration.
Pride of place is given to the long ears of barley which, in this case, are used complete with their lavish whiskers. In a smaller design, of course, they could be trimmed to fit the space. Other dried material is great water grass, like dark brown ostrich feathers, wild oats, long ears of Timothy grass resembling miniature, sun-bleached bulrushes, burdock burrs, white statice, stonecrop (sedum) and a single coral rosebud.
On the whole, dried materials have a matt finish and the gloss of preserved materials offers a welcome contrast in texture. The laurel leaves, glistening and nearly black, cast dark, friendly shadows; the rose hips, glycerine-preserved and then lacquered, are scattered singly and in pairs, and the beech husks, preserved on their branches, look like four-petalled wooden flowers.

Diagram 8 shows in detail how the design above the photograph is built up, with the top central motif a bunch of barley heads on either side of an equally prickly teasel. Follow the design to achieve a similar balance of texture and colour with the material in your collection.

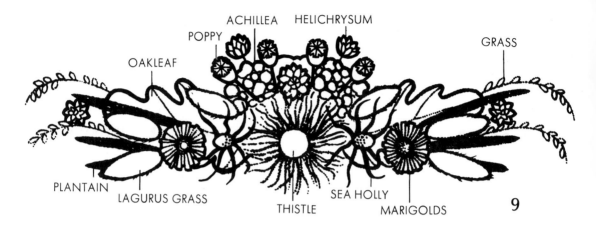

Hillside farm

If you want to use dried materials which are almost exactly the same colour as the background, make them show up by placing an intervening layer of a contrasting colour. In each of the four main motifs surrounding the hillside photograph, a pair of preserved oak leaves separates the pale creams and greens of the grasses and seedheads from the corn-coloured mount; a single, preserved ivy leaf, supporting sprays of dried nipplewort, gives strength and definition at each corner. All the other materials are dried.

In the central top motif (Diagram 9), a small pale golden thistle has a dried sea holly flower on each side of it and a fan of small poppy seedheads above. Note that the poppies are not set flat on their stalks but are resting on the crescent of dried yellow achillea behind them. Hare's tail grass heads and other grasses carry the design out beyond the oak leaves; they contrast well against the brown of the leaves and blend softly into the background beside them. More positive colour is provided by small pale pink helichrysum (straw daisy) flowers and orange marigolds. These were dried in a granular compound as described in Chapter 2.

The central group beneath the photograph repeats the thistle and sea holly motif. On either side there is a bunch of sycamore keys, a white helichrysum and an upward curving bunch of lavender. Two pink and one yellow helichrysum are set on the yellow achillea.

The two side decorations are identical and are again set on a pair of oak leaves. A bunch of white statice in the centre is surrounded by sprays of yellow achillea. Hare's tail grass and long frondy grass heads provide the width. Notice that the long grass is stuck only along the end of the stem; the seedheads stand away from the mount and cast interesting shadows. Two small sprays of hogweed, with its narrow pin stripes in deep red, illustrate well how a snippet from a giant plant can be used in small-scale designs. The decoration is completed with two poppy seedheads and two dried coral rosebuds.

Follow the diagrams for the detailed outline of the decorative motifs, adapting them to suit your materials. With a little imagination, things which look most unpromisingly large at first can be snipped down to size and made to blend into the scheme.

Chapter 9

The Shape of Things

As with many charming old customs which we have adopted, the use of pomanders, or "clove oranges", had an intensely practical application. In the fifteenth and sixteenth centuries—in the days before constant hot water and aerosol air fresheners—pomanders were carried about as a safeguard against infection and to cloak unwelcome household odours. Now, with their strong, pungent, spicy aroma, we use them to keep moths away from clothes and linen and, at the same time, to give us an occasional drift of fragrance like the scent of orange blossom on a Mediterranean breeze; or they are lovely just for decoration, for a clove-studded orange, dried to a tight little nut-brown ball, and garnished with trailing ribbons, is as pretty as a Christmas tree ornament.

To make a traditional pomander, choose a fully ripe orange with a thin skin. Bear in mind that the fruit will shrink considerably as it petrifies; one that is small to start with might become scarcely more than golfball sized in the course of time. As a variation, you can use a lemon or lime in the same way, but the orange is more usual.

Each orange will take about two small jars of whole cloves. For an even more evocative effect, you can first dip the cloves in a herb or flower oil extract. Many old-fashioned chemists and most herbalists sell one or two pure plant oils such as oil of thyme, rosemary, lemon, lavender or geranium. Or you can use one of the natural flower essences in the Mary Quant range—in this case choose from Spring Blossom, Country Garden, wistaria or honeysuckle. Shake the plant oil into a saucer and roll the cloves in it, turning them over so that the oil thoroughly impregnates them.

Press the cloves into the skin of the orange, as close together as possible. Work in circles, starting from the stalk end, until the surface of the orange is completely covered.

The next step, like the use of plant oil, is optional. You can strengthen the spiciness of the orange by rolling it in a mixture of 1 teaspoon dried orris root powder and 1 teaspoon ground cinnamon. Press the orange well into the powder so that it packs into the clove heads.

Wrap the orange in dark-coloured tissue paper and put it in a box to mature for two weeks, or three if the cloves were soaked in flower oil. You can wrap a handful of pot-pourri in the tissue; the orange and the petal mixture will each enhance the other.

Press an upholstery staple (or T-shaped pin) into the top of the orange, thread a narrow ribbon through and tie in a bow. Hang the pomander in a wardrobe, on a coat hanger or over your dressing table, or put it in a drawer to scent lingerie, linen and woollens.

Pomanders have been credited with other powers and advantages, as these verses from the poem *The Clove Orange* by Eleanor Farjeon tell:

I'll make a clove orange to give to my darling,
I'll make a clove orange to please my delight,
And lay in her coffer to sweeten her linen
And hang by her pillow to sweeten her night.

I'll choose a small orange as round as the moon is,
That ripened its cheek in the sunniest grove,
And when it is dry as a midsummer hayfield
I'll stick it all round with the head of a clove.

To spice the dull sermon in church of a Sunday,
Her orange of cloves in her bag she shall take;
When parson is prosy and eyelids are drowsy,
One sniff at her spice-ball will charm her awake.

And when she walks forth in the highways and byways
Where fevers are prone and infection is rife,
On her palm she shall carry her little clove orange,
A charm against sickness, to guard her sweet life.

And moth shall not haunt her most delicate garment,
Nor spectre her delicate dream in the night,
When she hangs in her chamber her little dried orange
I've studded with cloves to delight my Delight.

Decorated pomanders

For a variation of the pomander theme, retaining all the desirable properties yet enhancing the woody brownness, oranges can be decorated with rings or panels of cloves alternated with other small-scale natural materials. The colour photograph on page 27 shows three pomanders not immediately recognisable now as conventional clove oranges, yet still aromatic and almost ever-lasting. We have used the dried flower heads of natural and ginger-brown dyed glixia, one of the most miniature of flowers, the tight little clusters of santolina heads, furry hare's tail (lagurus) grass, helichrysum in parchment and orangey-brown colours and the beautiful autumnal beech husk. Other suitable materials would be trimmed barley or wheat ears, tiny poppy seedheads, the delicate mauvey-brown seedheads of love-in-a-mist, snipped off spikes of papery-thin dried bluebells—in fact, anything in your collection that is small in scale and contrasts well with the robust texture of the cloves.

When the orange is to be studded with other materials it is advisable to dry the fruit first. To do this, hang it in a warm, dry place, such as an airing cupboard, for two weeks before beginning the decoration.

An orange is easy enough to handle when you are studding it with cloves, but dried flowers and seedheads are more brittle and you will need to have the fruit held rigid in front of you as you work. Simply hanging it on a hook is a strain on the patience, as an irritating game of punch ball inevitably develops. A better way is to push a large ball of non-hardening modelling clay (Plasticine) or putty on to an old saucer and pierce the orange with a length of stout wire or knitting needle. Push the free end of the wire or needle into the holding material so that the fruit is held firm and

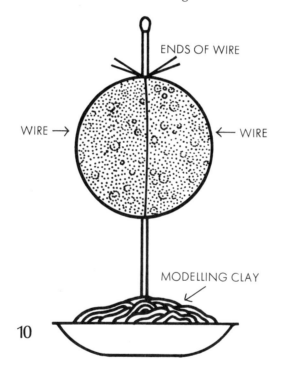

ENDS OF WIRE

WIRE →   ← WIRE

MODELLING CLAY

10

upright (Diagram 10). In this way, you can turn the saucer round to work on the other side of the fruit, and reverse the wire, pushing the fruit to the other end of it, to work on the underside.

To hang a pomander decoration you can push a staple into the top when the ball is finished, or bind the orange two or four times round with the narrowest ribbon, choosing a colour to tone with the natural materials of your decoration and making it part of the design. Depending on the type of design, the ribbon can be tied round the orange before or after decorating. Tie the ribbon firmly at the top, make a bow and leave two ends to make a loop for hanging.

When working a design in segment panels, rather than in rings round the fruit, it is a good idea to draw guide lines on the fruit first. The closeness of the work can become a little confusing.

When using dried materials on such a small scale, it is obviously unthinkable to wire each flower and seedhead—unless you want just one for a top or centre accent. Go through your collection first and choose those with firm, stout stalks. Grade for size flowers and other materials of the same type. Unless you want to make a virtue of size difference, discrepancies could look unplanned and untidy. Cut the stalks very short—about $\frac{1}{4}$-inch (7 mm) long at the most. Cloves will penetrate orange skin easily but most other materials will need help, particularly if you have dried the orange first. Pierce a hole for each stalk with a darning needle, making sure to push it straight into the skin if you want the material to rest flat on the surface of the fruit and at an angle only if you want the material to lean one way or the other.

Santolina rings

The main design point in the decoration with the rings of santolina heads (top right in the colour photograph on page 27) is the closely-packed effect of circles of different sizes and textures. They all hug the surface of the fruit tightly to keep the compact shape. Of the three pomander decorations, this is the only one that could be laid in a drawer; the others would suffer badly from such treatment.

Start by encircling the circumference of the orange with four tightly packed rings of cloves. On the side of the orange facing you, make a tight circle of the greeney-beige santolina heads—or other dried material of an appropriate size and colour—so that they overlap the cloves. Follow this with a "staggered" double row of glixia heads, even more delicate looking in their natural parchment colour. To do this, insert the first ring of flowers and arrange the second so that each flower comes between two in the first ring. Now make two more rings of cloves, another of santolina and fill in the centre of the circles with cloves. Pierce a hole in the centre and push in a fully-opened beech husk so that its silky "petals" almost cover the centre cloves. Turn the orange round and repeat the design on the reverse.

When it is completed, push a staple in the top and thread $\frac{1}{4}$-inch (7 mm) wide green ribbon through. Tie a double bow and make a loop with the trailing ends.

If you would like to display the pomander decoration, as we did, by setting it on a piece of pottery or a pretty teacup, there is no need to repeat the design on the reverse. Simply stud the other side with cloves.

Lagurus grass strips

To make the decoration with the wispy heads of lagurus or hare's tail grass (on the left in the colour photograph), begin by winding narrow white "baby" ribbon tightly four times round the orange. The ribbon will act as guide lines for the eight strips of grass heads. Fill in the panels between the ribbon with tightly packed rows of cloves. The neatest way to do this is to outline the pointed oval segments with rows of cloves and work inwards to the centre of each panel. You will probably have five or six cloves across at the widest part.

With a darning needle, pierce holes at intervals along the ribbon strips and push the grass heads in so that the grasses are touching but not crowded. The fat, furry shapes will hide the ribbon beneath them. If your collection does not include this type of grass, choose

82

something that would give a similar effect – snipped off heads of wheat, barley, oats or rye, or one of many different kinds of grass would be equally effective.

Remove one clove from the centre of each panel and push in an orange helichrysum (straw daisy) head. If the most perfect flower in your bunch has lost its stalk – as one of ours did – you can cheat and push a glass-headed pin through the centre. The enfolding petals will keep your secret. Turn the plate round and repeat the design on the other side of the orange – or just stud with cloves if you wish.

Straw daisy ring

For the third decorated pomander (in the foreground in the photograph), we used pale straw-coloured helichrysum and glixia flowers dyed ginger brown.

Begin by binding the orange once round with narrow white ribbon, securing it at the top. Tie the bow and loop later. Make a double row of cloves round the circumference of the fruit, close to the ribbon. Next, make a staggered double row of ginger glixia flowers, the stalks cut to about $\frac{1}{4}$-inch (7 mm) long. Follow that with about five tightly packed rows of cloves into the centre.

Pierce holes through the ribbon for the helichrysum, so that when they are inserted the flowers will just touch each other all round the ring and will hide the ribbon. Try the flowers against the fruit to judge the diameter before making the holes. Push the flowers in place. Pierce a hole in the centre of the panel of cloves and push in a large, flat flower head. Repeat the design on the reverse or, again, simply stud with cloves if the decoration is for a "flat" display. Tie the ribbon in a double bow and make a loop if needed for hanging.

If life seems too short to make something so unashamedly pretty just for yourself (but we think you should!) we can't imagine a more welcome gift for a friend, someone who is ill or elderly. And as Christmas tree decorations and presents these ornaments are unrivalled. One of the charming things about them – which we discovered quite by accident – is that the glixia flowers open up in the warmth of the firelight, just as so many flowers do in the heat of the summer sun.

Hanging ball

From decorated oranges to a hanging ball worked on a preformed plastic foam sphere. The technique is much the same, but there can be a wide variation in diameter, for these balls of foam can be bought in a range of sizes. They are effective in a number of ways; hanging several at different levels, as a "mobile"; low over a dining table or sidetable; in a doorway or, as we show in the photograph on page 28, in the curve of an arch.

The ball we used was about $4\frac{1}{2}$ inches (11–12 cm) in diameter. To work the decoration, stick a knitting needle through the ball and embed it in non-hardening modelling clay on a plate, as already described. As a guide line, and to facilitate hanging later, bind fine wire vertically round the circumference, leaving the ends free to make a loop for the ribbon. As you add the cones, the decoration tends to become very heavy. If it threatens to topple from the anchoring pin, build up a further mound of modelling clay until it is secure again. We chose a brown, white and silver colour scheme, carried out with tightly closed fir cones, sprigs of dried white statice, both preserved and dried senecio leaves, fluffy dried thistle heads and, a great asset, individual dried lupin pods.

You will find that preserved leaves of senecio are more supple and have soft, pliable stalks. Even when you pierce each hole in the foam first with a sharpened matchstick, which we recommend in any case, it is still difficult to push them in. The dried leaves are easier. You can use them on either side, with the grey or silver side out. We chose the silver underside and then echoed this tone in the Christmas packaging ribbon used for hanging.

We dried long spikes of the lupin pods upside down and were delighted with their progress. They developed from small, grey, pea-like pods to something with a very interesting personality. Each pod opened, discarded its seeds (a sheet of newspaper under the drying material is useful to avoid this waste) and then twisted into a pair of silvery-grey spirals. In this way, you see a fascinating contrast in colour and texture between the inside of the pod, a matt brownish-grey, and the furry outside. What is more, the pods are complete, each one with its own little stalk, so they push easily into the foam.

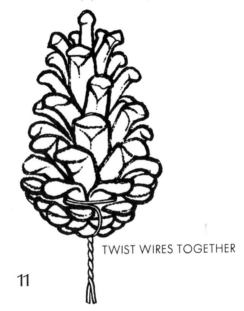

TWIST WIRES TOGETHER

11

If your cones do not have stalks, you will need to wire them; twist a 5-inch (13 cm) rose wire (or any other strong but pliable wire) round the next but last lower layer of the "petals". Wind the wire right round the cone, twist the two ends round each other tightly against the cone, then all the way down to form a stalk. Wired cones will not stay in the foam ball as well as those with natural stalks, particularly upside down; if you have some of each, use the natural ones at the bottom of the design and the wired ones at the top. Cut the natural stalks short, to a length of not more than about $\frac{3}{8}$ inch (10 mm).

We started the design with a row of lupin pods, following the placement of the vertical wire. Then, on either side of that, a row of cones; then statice, then senecio leaves, thistles and, at the sides of the design (as seen in the colour photograph) cones again. The design is identical on the other side.

To hang the ball, twist the free ends of wire to form a small loop and thread a length of ribbon or package tie through. Secure the join in the ribbon by sewing. If you like, you can tie an extra bow and attach it to the hanging ribbon, using a paper fastener or sewing it to secure.

84

Cone centrepiece

You can use all kinds of dried and preserved natural materials to decorate these foam shapes. From the cones, leaves and lupin pods of the hanging ball, we turn to beech husks, seedheads, rowan berries and white everlasting flowers in the cone shown on page 45.

The colour theme here is vaguely red, white and blue, all the colours subtle and muted. The red is represented by the rowan berries, the white by the dried everlasting flowers—use ammobium, rhodanthe, xeranthemum, helipterum, whatever you have in your collection —and the blue by the dried poppy seedheads. Preserved beech mast, complete with nuts, and dried love-in-a-mist seedheads provide a brownness which, in this scheme, acts as a neutral shade.

The pattern forms a helter-skelter shape down the cone and presents each row of natural material in an interesting light. The lines of seedheads etcetera are seen from almost every angle at once as they twist round and round the cone.

It is important that there should not be any show-through of the basic foam shape. Ours was green and in order not to take any chances—a flash of green would have spoiled the over-all colour impression—we painted the cone black. Show-through then just looks like a deep shadow. The foam material is, of course, highly porous and a 10-inch-high cone will take at least one small pot of black poster paint, mixed with a very little water in order not to dilute the colour. Alternatively, you can use black water colour in tube form. Leave the cone to dry completely. An airing cupboard speeds up the process, and while you are doing that, put in a ball of non-hardening modelling clay to soften it.

When the cone is dry, stick a drawing pin (thumb tack) into the top of it and wind a length of fine garden wire round and round in the spiral shape you want the design to follow—you can choose whether the spiral is "open" or "closed". This might not come just right the first time. Adjust it until it looks satisfactory, then twist the wire end under the cone and push it into the surface out of the way.

Stick the lump of softened modelling clay on to an old plate, push two matchsticks into the base of the cone and wedge them into the clay. This will keep the cone rigid while you work and enable you to turn it round as you proceed.

Using the wire as a guideline, insert the first row, from top to bottom and round and round the cone. Start with preserved beech husks with nuts. Use a sharpened matchstick to pierce a hole for each piece as you are ready to place it. Try the beech mast on the cone against the last one you inserted, so that you can tell exactly where the hole should be. They should just touch each other but, because of their bulk, cannot overlap.

Next, insert a closed row of rowan berries beneath the beech. Because these are the only really bright colour in the design, use as many as you can, making a staggered double row if you like.

Next come the urn-shaped poppy seedheads, inserted so that they touch each other at the widest part of the bulge. The seedheads are blue-grey, but their star-shaped tops are pale brown, a pretty contrast.

The next row is white everlasting flowers with bright sun-yellow centres. These give a blaze of crisp whiteness at the beginning of the row, near the top of the design, but bury their heads shyly beneath the overhanging poppy heads lower down.

The last row is made up of love-in-a-mist seedheads. Even from one packet of seed, these plants will produce seedheads in a wide range of colouring, some plain and some dramatically striped. We chose purpley-brown ones and saved a fine specimen, lavishly decorated, still with its wire-like foliage, for the top.

As the decoration is the same all round, and equally attractive viewed from whatever angle, it is ideal as a dining table centrepiece or on a table in the centre of a room. And as it is virtually everlasting, it can be carefully packed away in tissue paper and a box when the spring and summer flowers are in blossom, and brought out to fulfil its important role in the autumn and winter.

Door wreath
A ball, a cone and now a hoop. This type of decoration, shown on a sun-dappled wall, on page 46, gives a warm welcome on a front door and is a pleasant alternative to a traditional Christmas holly wreath. You can buy foam hoops but, in fact, we were unable to find one large enough when we needed it. And so instead we had a moss wreath made for a very nominal sum by a florist. It measured just over 1 foot (30 cm) in diameter and had a protective covering of dark green plastic, wound round and round like a shiny bandage.

It is easiest to work a wreath when it is hanging up. For one thing, you can better judge the effect of the materials as you are placing them, and for another you do not have to support the weight of it when you want to pull it away from the surface to place cones and other material towards the back. Fix a loop of strong doubled wire round the top of the hoop, twist it at the back and form it into a loop to hang.

The colour scheme is yellow and marmalade, lime green, white and brown–though the shades between the yellow and brown are subtle reflections of those two main colours, which dominate the all-over effect.

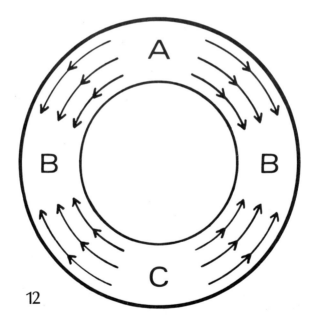

12

The materials in the wreath are false cypress (chamaecyparis), preserved in glycerine, small closed cones and the larger ones hanging at the base, white Australian mountain heather, araucaria grass, a muted shade of lime green, yellow everlasting flowers (again, use whichever you happen to have; the effect will be very similar) and a little preserved mistletoe. This, really, pays lip-service to the traditional materials of Christmas decorations.

The design is worked on the overlapping principle. To achieve a rhythm in the direction of the materials, work from a point at the top, A on Diagram 12, downwards towards the centre on each side, B; then start at the bottom, C, and work upwards on each side to B again. In this way, the leaves and other materials in the top half of the wreath will face upwards and those in the lower half hang downward.

Begin by wiring the large cones at the base of the design, taking the wire right round the frame.

As you work on each half of the wreath, keep checking that you are achieving an even distribution of the different materials, and a good balance of colours and textures.

If you like you can decorate the wreath with glass baubles and a large ribbon bow.

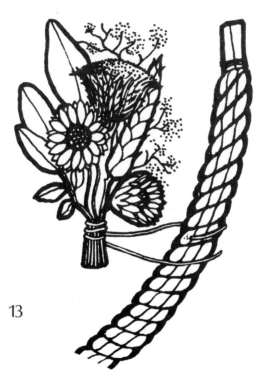

13

Garland

The most flexible shape of all is the garland, built around a length of cord. The decoration is shown in colour on page 47 in a jokey way, decorating a stone statue of a dog. It can be hung round a plaster or bronze figure, in a U-shape or even as a flat ribbon against a wall, in a hoop low over a dining table or, for that matter, flat on a large table as a centre-piece for a buffet party.

You can use dressing gown cord as we did, any other thick cord, coarse string or rope with a diameter of about $\frac{5}{8}$-inch (15 mm). If your material is narrower than this, twist two or more lengths to make tightly wound cord of the suggested thickness. To do this twist the cord as tight as possible in the direction of its natural twist and double it back on itself. Tie each end with wire, make a loop with the wire on one end and hang it on to a drawing pin (thumb tack) pressed into a vertical surface, such as the edge of a shelf. To make a hanging ribbon, work on the cord in this position.

To make a garland, push another drawing pin into the vertical surface, about 6 inches (15 cm) away from the first, form a loop with the wire securing the second end of the cord, and hang this from the drawing pin. The cord will now be in a U-shape. When you have completed the design, you can wire the two ends together to make a hoop. You must measure the cord and shape it as described while it is still pliable, before you decorate it with flowers and leaves.

The scheme we chose was in the spring-like colours of crocus flowers—mauve, yellow, white and blue. As you need only snippets of the material, with stalks no longer than about $1\frac{1}{2}$ inches (4 cm), this is an ideal design to use up all the trimmings and clippings you will have collected while working on other decorations.

We used mauve thistle heads, lavender, yellow achillea, everlasting flowers in mauve, yellow and white, hare's tail grass, senecio leaves, sea lavender and preserved bay leaves. The easiest way to attach the materials to the cord is to gather them in your hand into little bunches of four or five pieces, according to size and width, and wire them together (Diagram 11). Trim the stalks so that they are even in length and wire each bunch to the cord. If you are making a flat ribbon, work from the top downwards, so that the posies will overlap upwards. For a garland, work from the top downwards on each side, meeting in the middle of the loop at the bottom. Try to make the design as three-dimensional, round and fat as possible, by wiring in bunches which will face out towards the sides. Check that no wires are showing. If they are, wire on a round shape, such as a thistle head or spray of achillea, to cover up.

To finish the garland, wire the two ends together and then add one or two more sprays to conceal the join.

Chapter 10

Choosing Containers

No-one talks about vases now, unless they are referring to works of art. The range of receptacles to hold flowers is so wide that the word would not nearly cover it. Containers can be anything, whether they can hold water or not, whether they are hollow or not, and whether they are decorative or not. For a container can be deliberately part of the design, a main feature of the arrangement, or simply a means of supporting the plant material and completely hidden by it.

It is interesting to note the development of the container in works of art. In early sixteenth century paintings, such as "A Vase of Flowers" by Ambrosius Bosschaert, and a design in Damascus tiles made in Iznik, Turkey, at the same time, the craft of the glass blower and the potter was portrayed with reverence, with the flowers a well-chosen accessory.

By the seventeenth century we have the flowers as the subject of the title. "Flowers in a Vase" by Willem van Aelst shows a graceful curve of full-blown roses, carnations and other summer flowers in a vase in shadow; another painting with the same title, by Jan van Huysum, shows a profusion of late spring blooms tumbling over an earthenware urn, with only one shaft of light striking the vase.

Renoir in his "Spring Flowers" created one of the most perfect harmonies between flowers and container, the whole painting a soft statement in white, the palest blue and, for the wallflowers, a light touch of coral. Similarly, in his sunflower paintings, Van Gogh chose the simplest of vases, the top half just the colour of the palest flowers so that again flowers and container have that made-for-each-other look.

By studying the works of great artists, perhaps we can all hope to develop a sense of fitness between container and plant material, without becoming too involved or scientific in our approach. For, after all, any flower arrangement is a very personal creation; it is much more important that it should please the arranger than simply conform to rule.

A modern American observer, Emma Hodkinson Cyphers, in her book, *Modern Abstract Flower Arrangements*, defines a container thus: "A vase may be a cylinder, a bowl may be a sphere, but the majority of containers are derived from cylinders expanded outward or contracted inward, or as spheres stretched upwards or downwards, or they are seen as a combination fused into a single form. These pulls and pushes, expansions and contractions sometimes are manipulated to produce free-form containers as well as geometric ones."

A pleasing design and a good relationship between container and plant material can be said to depend on proportion; without sticking to hard and fast rules, it is nevertheless important to achieve this balance. In Victorian England arrangements tended to concentrate equally on plant material and container, but most of us today find this half-and-half split of interest uncomfortable. In fact, even without thinking about it (and this, surely, is the way to arrive at what basically pleases us) we tend to employ a formula discovered by a Greek mathematician, Eudoxos, in 350 BC. This might, indeed, be one of the earliest pieces of market research, because Eudoxos, in order to find the secret of perfect proportion, asked his friends to mark on a length of stick the point they found most interesting. Their entirely non-scientific judgment gave a fascinating result: that it is a point two thirds from one end and one third from the other which holds the most interest. Interpreted to flower design, this would mean that the most pleasing proportions would result when the height of the container or width of the base was one third of the total height of an arrangement.

When one is learning to design with flowers and other plant material, and finds that a grouping looks wrong, it is usually because this proportion is not followed. This is why it is easier to start a design by placing the material which gives the height and the width and determines the relationship of the plant material to the container.

Staffordshire angel

An arrangement becomes not just a pleasure, but quite a responsibility when the container is a work of art in its own right. Relationship between container and contents is never of greater consequence. The holder must be studied carefully for colour, size, shape and, more important, "feeling" and the arrangement be a complementary understatement. It will probably help if you make a rough sketch of the container and pencil in a number of shapes for the arrangement until the right balance is achieved.

> We chose a Staffordshire group of an angel and two young girls and adorned it with natural materials in soft, unassuming colours, the main one being, appropriately, pale heavenly blue. The photograph on page 48 shows the result.
>
> The aperture, no more than 4 by $1\frac{1}{4}$ inches (10 by 3 cm), imposed restrictions not only of size but also of accessibility. It is not possible to work from the back of the group, and there is not much room for fingers to move freely in front of it.
>
> The shallow recess was first filled with a mound of white non-hardening modelling clay; then the surface pierced with a sharpened matchstick until it looked like the top of a

pepperpot. This helped to push in the more flexible stems.

The shape, a softly curving S, was outlined first, with a spray of preserved bay leaves at the top and a fern leaf, preserved in glycerine, on the right. The main colour statement was made by the deep blue hydrangea florets, the deepest colour retention of all the ones we treated, the pale blue-mauve of the clematis heads and, of course, the lavender. Three tiny sprigs of dried yellow achillea are used to resemble rays of bright sunshine in a summer sky. Neutral colouring comes from the leaf sprays of dried santolina, briza maxima grass heads and the globe thistle (echinops), full of depth and interest. Colour strength is there in the preserved blackberry leaves, one triple spray of pressed blackberry leaves, and the bobbly heads on the lino grass, effectively and dramatically dyed black.

Containers from Nature

The colour photograph on page 57 shows how well dried and preserved materials complement a natural container, in this case two large sea shells. Even tiny shells found by the sea or river can hold small nosegays of minute spring flowers, making the very most of the first snowdrops, aconites or violets.

> The large shell, a triton (Charonia pustulata), was filled with white Plasticine (non-hardening clay) to within about one inch of the rim. This is a suitable holding material for all but the flimsiest stems because it adheres well to the container and gives good rigidity.
> The design is based on the slightly curving S shape outlined with sprays of pale silvery green sea holly (eryngium), harmonising well both in colour and texture with the ridged sea shell. On the left of the longest sprays, and still following the top curve, there are sprays of dried bluebell (Scilla nutans) the colour and almost the texture of fine parchment, graded for height to give a crescent shape.
> The colour of the sea holly is repeated in the dried hydrangea flower heads, placed to come above and slightly below the rim of the shell. This colour is followed through again by the large thistles which, of course, darken progressively to a deep purple.
> One large preserved oak leaf gives weight and depth on the left side, balancing the largest of the thistles opposite and is covered by frondy sprays of dried sea lavender or marsh rosemary (limonium), an everlasting with loose sprays of small violet flowers.
> The central and focal point of the design is provided by a group of coral-coloured roses, dried in a chemical preparation (Chapter 2). In the smaller shell, designed as an accessory to the larger one on a white marble table top, two small but well-opened thistles provide weight at the rim, some florets have been cut from a pale green dried hydrangea and the outline shape provided by sprays of sea holly and pale green rue seedheads. Notice how effective the spider-like outline of a sea holly flower is when seen from directly above.

Driftwood makes a most attractive, natural support for dried material, showing the leaves and flowers in a near-realistic setting. Those living far inland need not despair: the term applies to wood weathered by the elements and not necessarily washed up by the sea for some lucky beachcomber to find. The wood might be large or small chunks of bark chipped from tree trunks or branches, portions of tree stumps or roots, or broken-off branches. Look on a country walk for any piece of wood that has an interesting shape and, if possible, a natural hollow which could support a pinholder, other holding material, a tin or jar.

To treat the wood, first scrub it gently to remove any insect life and dirt; wood with a silvery-grey coating should be treated with extra care so that you do not also remove the surface. Trim the wood of any out-of-balance projections that spoil the shape, and scrape out any areas of soft wood. If you want to achieve a dull, smooth appearance, rub with sandpaper; but take care not to detract from the natural woodland or seashore look that is part of its value. Dry the wood in the sun or in a warm, airy place. Check that the piece will stand level and firm; a branch gently swaying in the breeze is one thing, but one that rocks to and fro once you have entrusted it with an arrangement of flowers and leaves is quite another. If necessary, sandpaper, file or saw it straight at the base.

To darken the wood, use brown, dark red or mahogany coloured shoe polish. To blacken it, hold it in the embers of a bonfire or the flame of a blow lamp. Black shoe polish gives a less realistic

and natural effect. To bleach driftwood, stand it overnight in a bucket containing a strong bleach solution. Rinse it well, then leave to dry.

Grey wood should not be polished, but other pieces can be given a coating of wax polish. To do this, brush on the wax, working it well into the wood, and leave for at least a day. Polish with a soft cloth.

Parts of coconut shells, too, make good containers for dried plant material. They have to be levelled off at one surface so that they will stand well, then, like a cornucopia, they can spill out an abundance of good things.

From large coconut shells, right down the scale to small broken eggshells. These can look endearingly pretty filled with a small posy of dried rose buds, miniature roses, pinks, delphinium florets, sweet peas or other tiny flowers. The eggshell can stand in a porcelain or pottery eggcup, or rest on a silver napkin ring.

Natural materials such as slabs of slate or granite, a cross-cut section of a tree trunk or even a large, flat preserved leaf are good stands for decorative arrangements, giving width at the base. Granite chippings, gravel, pebbles, stone, tiny shells, sand, rock, bark, coral, fungi, moss and even coal are good cover-ups for the mechanics supporting a design, and, if cleverly used, do not look like "screens" at all. Natural accessories standing beside an arrangement, and an integral part of the balance and proportion, can include fir cones, a handful of nuts, beech mast, dried ornamental gourds or polished stones.

Wooden bucket arrangement

Not natural wood, exactly, but the natural look of an old wooden butter carrier, gives a rural feeling to the arrangement shown in colour on page 58. The display brightens up a dark corner of a country kitchen and softens the clinical look that inevitably creeps in with the rows of gleaming appliances. Other interesting containers in this context would be a wooden trug or flower basket, cane fruit bowl, rush basket, even a shopping basket.

The wooden carrier has a handle, but as it is articulated it can be stored behind the vessel. An inner container, a large coffee tin, is filled with dry, clean silver sand; instead, the container could be partly filled with sand or dry gravel and a block of artificial holding material pushed into the top.

The colour scheme was dictated by the pale eucalyptus green of the working surface and the pine cupboard fronts. It is a study, therefore, in cream, pale brown and soft greyish green, a cool and restful theme, ideal for a room which is a hub of activity.

The height in the design is provided by large, fluffy sprays of pampas grass (Cortaderia), picked when not quite fully developed, first dried and then sprayed with ordinary hair spray to prevent the seeds from shedding. With thick-stemmed materials such as this, it is helpful to cut the stems slantwise before pushing them into the holding material; though in the case of sand, of course, this is not necessary.

One of the most delightful garden flowers to grow specially for preserving is Bells of Ireland (Molucella). The variety M. laevis is a particularly good one for arranging, growing as it does to a height of 2 feet. The leaves were first removed, the stems preserved in glycerine and then hung upside down to dry. During this process the calyces ripen from bright green to a creamy-ivory colour.

For the long, straight stems alternating with the pampas grass and Bells of Ireland, any kind of dried ornamental grass or corn would be suitable. From your collection, choose ears of wheat or barley and grasses which contrast with each other – some soft and fluffy, others long and spiky.

The sprays of hops used in the arrangement were dried by hanging upside down; this process leaves them somewhat brittle; they can be preserved in glycerine, in which case the colour will be darker.

As a focal point, and providing the solid round shapes of the design, there are several heads of hydrangea, dried by standing the stems in a little water. Our collection happened to include the gift of a cluster of deep cream dried berries brought back by a friend from a foreign holiday; without these, another large hydrangea head would suffice.

A group of dried ornamental gourds has been added to the arrangement as an accessory, extending the width of the design and echoing the colour theme, though in deeper tones.

Raisin jar

Photographed on page 59 against a timbered wall in the same kitchen, a white Victorian raisin jar makes a strikingly simple container for a cluster of dried flowers and grasses. Old, weathered timber often has a deep mauvish-brown colour, and this has been perfectly matched in the depth of colour of the love-in-a-mist seedheads which are a main feature of the arrangement.

The jar is filled with artificial holding material to within about one inch of the top, then a layer of non-hardening clay (Plasticine) is pushed in to form a collar round the inside of the rim. This helps to hold the smaller and more delicate stems securely.

The seedheads of love-in-a-mist or Devil-in-a-bush (Nigella damascena) are at least as pretty as the cornflower blue, pink, mauve and white flowers they bear in the summer. The seedheads range in colour from pale parchment to deep mauve-brown, and some are attractively flashed with both colours. The heads are dried by hanging and retain the fine, soft, feathery foliage along the stems.

The outline of the design was made with the longest stems of these seedheads, some light and some dark-coloured. A second and third ring was placed, in descending height, to make almost a fan shape of the dried material.

Sprays of dried Russian vine (Polygonum baldschuanicum) are interspersed among the stems, covering what would otherwise be a background of splaying lines. The vine, the most trailing of the material used, hangs over the tim of the raisin jar just enough to obscure the top of the container. White and pale cream helichrysum (straw daisies) are grouped in and around the centre of the arrangement, masking the mass of stems.

Lastly, there are the soft, feathery heads of hare's tail grass (lagurus), the stems cut to long, medium and short lengths. For the best effect, choose some heads that have a natural curve or twist and others that stand in a straight line with the stem. Even this variation in the formation of the grass seedhead adds to the interest of the arrangement. If you have difficulty in inserting the last of the stems in the rim of clay, because of the closeness of the other materials, use a pair of tweezers to help you.

There is no place in a "utility" room for fussy arrangements or ornate containers, but where simplicity can be maintained, a decoration can play a vital role. Other suitable containers would be ginger jars, old stone or earthenware pots, enamel or white china jugs, dark brown ovenware casseroles or copper or brass kitchenware (see Chapter 12).

Bathroom windowsill

For a small modern bathroom, you need the most unpretentious arrangement possible, one that doesn't look extravagant when space has to be measured in inches, like the one on page 60.

The container, a pottery mug with warm brown glazes, holds a medley of a countryside harvest. The mechanics: a block of dry holding material almost filling the mug and a collar of non-hardening modelling clay round the rim.

The preserved ivy leaves all came from the same vine, a piece about seven feet long, but have shown their individuality by emerging in colours ranging from pale honey to khaki green. After they had been preserved in glycerine solution the leaves were polished with a little cooking oil on cottonwool, until they shone to rival the glaze itself for highlights.

The spikes of seedheads, some a pale greenish colour and some a creamy-beige, are dried wild foxglove. Cultivated varieties would give much the same results, but tend to be larger. One fluffy thistle head and a clump of old man's beard provides the softness in the scheme, a feeling which is carried through in the outlines of the stipa grass at the back.

The dried thistle-like material, Australian dryandra, presents a completely matt surface, a fine contrast to the glistening ivy; also from Australia, the sprigs of dried heather.

The sprays of wild blackberries almost look as if they had been used straight from a country walk; but they were first stripped of their leaves and then preserved in anti-freeze solution. To restore some of their original gloss you could polish them with cooking oil. For a defiant touch of winter colour there are a few pieces of lemon yellow forsythia, dried for two days in preserving crystals (see Chapter 2).

Chapter 11

Arrangements in Miniature

Designs in miniature are just like any other flower arrangements, but simply on a smaller scale. The proportion of container to natural materials; the balance of shiny and dull textures; the relationship of light and dark colours, all the general remarks apply and must be taken into account. Miniature arrangements are usually understood to be those not exceeding six inches in width, and so it is obvious that placement of these designs needs careful thought. They are ideal for a dressing table, where they can be seen in scale with scent bottles and cosmetic jars, on a small wine table or beside a place setting at dinner or tea; but you clearly cannot expect a single arrangement to make an impact alone in the middle of a vast piece of furniture. For this reason, miniatures are often designed in sets, perhaps three at a time, so that together on a table or shelf they form a related group of individual components, each with characteristics of its own.

Looking round for miniature containers becomes almost a new hobby and the possibilities are endless. When it is to be used for dried and preserved materials, the article does not even have to be able to contain water or dampened holding material. Consider tiny snuff or pill boxes—bearing in mind that, once the lids are opened, the containers practically double in size—ink wells, salt cellars, scent bottles, egg cups, china spoons, candle snuffers, thimbles, bottle or decanter stoppers, even doll's house furniture. You can use dry holding material if the container has an aperture, but a ball or collar of non-hardening modelling clay will often be more satisfactory to secure the delicate stalks.

Tweezers are useful for handling the material, and manicure scissors the right size for snipping it into shape.

To be in scale with the small containers, the plant material does not have to start life in miniscule form. Small flowers such as glixia, snowdrops, buttercups, daisies and so on inevitably spring to mind, but there are many compound flowers or sprays of leaves which can be broken down into separate parts. A hydrangea floret is scarcely any larger than a buttercup; one larkspur flower much the same size as a double snowdrop, and so on. Achillea flower heads, which form such large umbrella-shaped clusters on the plant, can be snipped into the tiniest clumps, honesty petals used like single raindrops; long spikes of rue seedheads divided up into a bounty of tiny star shapes: look at your plant collection with fresh eyes and you will see miniature material in practically everything.

Green glass set

Two green glass bottles make the three containers seen in colour on page 61—the larger one has a decorative ring round the neck and the smaller one makes two tight little posies, in both the bottle and the upturned stopper, completing the trio. The materials used in the three containers are not identical, but linked by a colour theme—white, yellow, silver and two shades of blue.

The larger jar measures $5\frac{1}{4}$ inches (just over 13 cm) high to the top of the stopper. It might have held smelling salts or some other medicament; indeed, might still, because the flower ring does not hinder its use.

The mechanics for the ring are simple—merely a long sausage shape in a dark toning colour of non-hardening modelling clay pressed to form a ring against the neck of the jar. For a design of this size, you will need a strip of clay about $\frac{3}{8}$-inch (10 mm) wide and $\frac{1}{4}$-inch (7 mm) thick.

All the material in this design is dried, the stalks cut to a length of more than $\frac{1}{4}$-inch (7 mm). There are the fluffy outlines of the clematis seedheads (this was a cultivated variety, but old man's beard would give much the same effect), the flat snippets of achillea providing the bright golden yellow, sprays of white statice, separate florets of larkspur, a rich mauvey-blue, and heads of briza maxima grass, like puffed out ears of wheat.

Press the clematis seedheads into the clay collar first, spacing them equally round the jar and leaving gaps between them. Fill these gaps with larkspur and statice, trimming the sprays so that they sit neatly in place. Press a ring of briza maxima grass heads round the bottom of the clay ring and push the tiny pieces of achillea all round the top, making sure that they cover the clay completely.

The smaller jar is only 3 inches (7·5 cm) high and, seen from above, is almost hidden by the cluster of dried materials in moonlight colours. This scheme is a diluted version of the flower ring, the hydrangea florets, a much paler blue than the larkspur, the single honesty seedhead petals like splashes of silver light, and the sprays of dried thyme and Russian vine only just off-white.

Wedge a ball of modelling clay into the top of the jar and shape it into a rounded dome rising well above the rim. This gives you a larger surface to insert the stalks. Pierce the dome all over with a sharpened matchstick or a cocktail stick until it looks like the top of a pepperpot.

Snip the dried materials into pieces of a suitable size and cut the stalks to about 1 inch (2·5 cm) long. Cover the dome with the hydrangea florets, placing them evenly all round the rim and close together over the top. If you have difficulty in inserting the fragile stems, roll the tiniest ball of clay on to the end of each stem, and using the matchstick again, push it into one of the ready-made holes.

Push honesty seedheads between the hydrangea florets, so that some will be seen full-face and some sideways on, whichever way the design is viewed. Complete the design with short sprays of thyme and Russian vine, cutting them so that their spikiness emerges just beyond the other materials.

The stopper has a rounded top. To make it stand firm upside down, roll a small ball of the clay and push it firmly against the glass. Invert the stopper and push a ball of modelling clay into the opening, again forming it into a mound. Pierce holes with a small stick.

Continuing the overall colour scheme, the stopper holds more larkspur florets, the tiny buds of the everlasting flowers, xeranthemum, dried senecio leaves and a few buds, pressed silver-grey santolina leaves and dried rue seedheads. These were cut early in their development and hung upside down to dry. Captured at this stage, they retain a soft greeny-yellow colour. Those left to dry on the plant turn a dark brown and don't even look as if they belong to the same family.

First, and using tweezers, make a ring round the rim with the larkspur flowers, pushing the stalks in as firmly as you can. Below these, but not so close together, insert a few of the everlasting flower buds, and above the larkspur, press in a tight double row of rue seedheads. Complete the Victorian posy effect with an xeranthemum flower in the centre, then fill in the design with tiny sprays of senecio and santolina leaves.

Shelf set

There could scarcely be a more varied selection of containers than the ones shown in colour on page 62, yet the choice of materials, all in neutral shades with just a hint of pale pink, unifies them into a set.

The sparkling white Victorian eggcup at the back, almost like a miniature urn, holds lupin pods, clusters of hogweed seeds, the little four-sectioned seedheads of rue, some in the palest green and some in buff colour, and silver and pink everlasting flowers.

Fill the eggcup with a mound of non-hardening modelling clay, not quite as high and rounded as an egg, and pierce it with holes. Set in the strongest material first, in this case the lupin seedheads. Fill in between them with the flat material which will hide the clay – the hogweed and everlasting flowers. Choose curving sprays of the rue seedheads so that they drape over the rim of the container and extend beyond the shape outlined by the lupins.

A beautiful object in its own right, the Victorian travelling inkwell takes quite happily to the addition of a few flowers. It would be an elegant decoration for a small writing table or could form part of a group, with other accessories, on a larger desk. Even without such an elegant container, you can build this kind of design around a miniature box of any kind, a small square candleholder or even an old book, such as a small dictionary.

The inkwell is filled with black ink, which proves a strong contrast to the pale colours of the natural materials, and, indeed, to the brass rim, lid and screw.

Stick a piece of modelling clay on to the rim, choose light, but not too delicate materials for the decoration. It was not possible in this case to pierce holes into the clay – it resulted only in lifting up the entire rim!

We chose one pale green Bells of Ireland flower head as a central feature. Used in such a small-scale design, where it is seen practically in close-up, the veins and the fawny-pink centre seem to become magnified.

A few bluebell heads, dried papery thin, and two small sprays of the seedheads of Samolus valerandi (which look rather like nipplewort seedheads and are shown draping over the side of the inkwell) provide roundness in the design and two minute sprays of cocksfoot grass the featheriness. Colour comes from the coral-pink helichrysum flowers and the small rosehips.

The decoration in a china spoon shows how effective a miniature display can be in an elongated article. If all your spoons are on the table when an Eastern dish is on the menu, copy the idea and build the design around something else, a cheese scoop, marrow spoon, a pipe or a pair of grape scissors, for example.

Choose a selection of materials from your own store, balancing shiny and matt textures, round and frondy shapes. Here again you can use the smallest snippets you have left.

Fill the bowl of the spoon with a mound of modelling clay, or fix the clay near the end of your chosen container. If the mound is large enough, pierce holes with a sharpened matchstick to make it easier to push in the delicate stalks.

We used two heads of Australian dryandra, almost thistle-like in their spiky roundness; all the other materials appear to radiate from this central feature. There are tiny white glixia flower heads, some of them framing the dryandra and some extending beyond the bowl of the spoon, and tiny clippings of preserved cupressus, now looking like little brown Christmas trees and strongly etched against the pale cream background of the shelf. A few sprigs of stonecrop, some dried santolina flowerheads and the shiny surface of the glycerined ivy leaf repeat the brownness; the pale green hydrangea florets and the single soft pink everlasting flower look like positive accents of colour. Over the handle of the spoon, and bringing it into the scheme of things, there are waving sprays of one of the lightest, airiest of grasses, Deschampsis caespitosa.

Candlestick and snuffer

Any meal would seem like a banquet with a table arrangement like this, a silver candlestick with a snuffer decorated as an accessory (see page 63).

The plant materials have been chosen so that they almost melt into the elegance of the container; a perfect complement of pale grey greens and silver, with only the helichrysum flowers as bright as the candle flame.

Although the design surrounds the candle there is very definitely a "right side", where all the interest is. Any candleholder on a stand can be used to copy the shape of the arrangement; or you could even make up a holder using a pretty plate or saucer.

Surround the candle with a 1-inch (2·5 cm) deep collar of modelling clay and push another mound on to the dish to hold the main weight of the design.

We picked all traces of mauve from the thistle heads until they looked like luxuriously soft, shiny shaving brushes, and arranged them three in a cluster and one at a lower level. Close against the base of the candle there are silvery honesty seedheads and tiny dried santolina flowers, while at the back and towards the front the extremes of height and width are stated by pressed fern leaves. Sprigs of silvery green lavender leaves and exuberant sprays of statice weave in and out of the thistles, and the pink helichrysum flowers are placed one in shadow at the front and one where it can bask in the candlelight. The shape of the candleholder is repeated in the long, curving piece of pressed yarrow leaf in the snuffer. Little is needed beside this: just a single thistle head and a few sprigs of lavender leaves and statice.

Chapter 12

Reflected in Copper and Brass

The warm, glowing autumn colours of dried leaves and the pale, papery quality of some dried flowers all have this in common: they are seen at their best in brass or copper containers. These bright, shiny metals catch every last ray of sun or lamplight, and draw attention naturally to the arrangement. They are particularly appropriate as decorations in the kitchen and harmonise perfectly with old or period-style furniture, especially oak.

Practically any discarded household metalware can be used to hold arrangements. Hollow articles like moulds, pans, scoops and measures, of course, seem made for the purpose, but even those that are not – saucepan lids, finger plates, trays, pestles and weights – can be used as bases, stands or accessories.

Collecting copper and brass for flower containers is a fascinating hobby in itself. Bargain-hunting in junk shops, country sale rooms and scrap metal merchants' yards is still rewarding if you are not looking for perfection. It will not matter if a skillet has lost its handle, a mould has a serious crack or split or only one of a set of wine or spirits measures is on offer; you can transform the article and give it a new and everlasting lease of life with leaves, grasses and flowers from your collection.

Window arrangement

Copper and brass ware which was originally in use in the kitchens of large country and town houses seems to have a particular affinity with preserved berries, fruits and herbs. The colour photograph on page 64 shows a brass scoop in its element, filled with rosemary, blackberries, rowan berries and rose hips; to a two-hundred-year-old kitchen utensil it must seem like old times! It is shown here in the kitchen of an old farmhouse.

In this arrangement, the height is provided by five sprays of rosemary (Rosmarinus officinalis) grouped together into a narrow column. The herb was preserved in a half-and-half mixture of motor car anti-freeze fluid and water (see Chapter 4); this treatment turns the stems silvery grey and leaves a deep blue-mauve. After several months, there is a tendency for the leaves to deepen further to blue-brown, still an attractive contrast to the light-coloured stems.

The blackberries, in two long sprays, were preserved by the same method. The fruit partially dries out and loses a little size and gloss, but remains essentially berry-like, providing one of the most interesting textures in preserved materials. The blackberry leaves are silver on the underside and deep brown on the face.

The rose hips, sprays of rowan (Sorbus) leaves and berries and bright yellow fruits of the holly were treated for about one week in a solution of anti-freeze and water. Colour retention in the fruits is good, but partial loss of moisture and withering is inevitable. However, painting or spraying with a clear lacquer after treatment does improve preservation. After a time the yellow berry fruits of the holly (Ilex Bacciflava) deepen to a gold tinted with amber, with the leaves a well-contrasting yellow-brown. Further interesting texture is provided by slender twigs of silver birch, with both the small young leaves and the catkins turning a pale nut brown after treatment in glycerine solution.

The rhododendron sprays were preserved complete with young, tightly furled buds. After treatment in glycerine both buds and leaves are tough and papery; the buds yellow-brown and the leaves still green but flashed with dark brown. The large spiky yellow leaves of Helleborus corsicus have a tendency to crinkle and look rather squashed after treatment in glycerine mixture. If this happens, it is easily and quickly remedied by holding the leaves over the steam from a kettle for a few moments. They will emerge shiny and supple again.

The two large leaves of fatsia japonica, giving width and weight on each side of the arrangement, were preserved in glycerine solution and, like the Helleborus corsicus, emerge in shades of yellow, olive green and brown. Fatsia leaves treated in a solution of anti-freeze and water remain just as soft but take on a deeper colouring.

Behind the rosemary, at medium height, are two examples of maple (acer) leaves, one yellow coloured and the other deep coppery brown. The leaves were preserved in glycerine solution. The copper one retained its suppleness, but the yellow one became slightly brittle and needed steaming.

Covering the handle of the pan there is a long spray of glycerined ivy (Hedera). In order to achieve the desired shape, with long, gentle curves, the stem was lightly bound with florist's wire. With shorter sprays, or where the stem was to be used in an upright position, this would not be necessary.

The mechanics for an arrangement of this type have to be firm enough to support both long and thick stems. A pinholder in the base of the pan supports a block of artificial holding material. This is covered with crumpled chicken wire. For extra security, this can be wired to the pan.

Any shallow, dished piece of copper would be suitable for an arrangement of this kind — a frying pan, saucepan, rice scoop, or the pan from a pair of balance scales. If the container has a side handle, the design should incorporate the handle and partly overlap it. In the design photographed, the outline is almost an equal triangle with the dominant colour, provided by the red berries, carried in a straight line down the centre and out to each side.

Samovar display

A lovely old samovar, such as the one shown in the colour photograph on page 73, is a thing of beauty in itself. However, few of us would use one these days for its original purpose, to serve tea, and it is an ideal container for a large and rather dramatic display of dried material.

The container was filled with a block of artificial holding material and the outline shape put in first with ears of dried corn – oats and barley in this case. Between the corn, and softer in silhouette, are long sprays of dried sea lavender.

An inner circle of large dried poppy seedheads, as pale in colour as the corn, provides the third significant shape: after straight lines and sprays of small papery flowers, now clearly defined rounds.

Depth of colour is given, diagonally across the arrangement, by the sprays of glycerine-preserved mahonia leaves, the chestnut brown of the lower ones almost blending in with the colour of the copper itself. On the left, a spray of beech leaves, also preserved in glycerine, as a point of interest: it is complete with a cluster of partly opened husks.

The dried creamy-green seedheads of giant hogweed, like showers of falling rain, are the central focal point; they are also taken outwards to the edge of the design.

Next to these, there are the parchment-coloured spikes of dried thistles and around them, in tight clusters extending to the back of the arrangement, the dried ripe seedheads of stonecrop (sedum). This plant, which has a mass of pink flowerheads in the summer and autumn, is a subtle pinky-grey when dried.

Like clouds of smoke behind the stonecrop are sprays of smoke tree which, in this design, echo the soft, muted feeling of the tapestry screen background.

The only bright colour is the rich burnished bronze of the dried helichrysum (straw daisies). Since these flowers are, in fact, the smallest of the material used, several are needed to make an impact.

Follow the photograph for shape and outline and substitute plant material from your collection which will give the same general effect.

Watering can

So much for arrangements and designs for the house, but what of the great outdoors? If we welcome our visitors in a porch beyond the front door, eat on the terrace, have drinks in a covered patio, spend leisurely family hours in an informal garden room, then all these areas deserve something of the attention to detail and the little finishing touches we lavish on the other rooms. An informal friendly looking display of natural materials provides instant softness, yet lasts season after season and doesn't demand constant daily or weekly renewal or attention.

As an example, we chose to show a design of mainly dried material in an old brass watering can. You can see it in the colour photograph on page 74, where the container has caught the depth of the evening sun and taken on the extra warmth of copper. Again, junk yard or scrap yard finds are ideal. If you can spot a gnarled old bucket, perhaps one that once belonged to a workman, an iron cooking pot or cauldron, a decorative piece of lead pipe, anything that looks right mid-way between the house and the garden, build your design around it.

It is not worth trying to make an arrangement of this kind without using some form of "mechanics". The long stems will just fall sideways and ruin everything.

The whole cavity of the watering can was filled with a dry artificial holding material; crumpled chicken wire or even dry sand could be used instead and would be more practical in a larger container. There is a block of the holding material in the mouth of the can and a rim, round the aperture, of non-hardening modelling clay (Plasticine).

The height of the design is outlined first by the dried bulrushes of the reed mace, and then by the browny sprays of great water grass. On the right, a criss-crossing pattern of the seedheads of corn-on-the-cob (maize) is used naturally just as it grows, to look as if it is being blown first this way and then that in the wind. Cock's foot grass makes neater, straighter outlines and teasels give weight and side definition.

The central feature, like any child's painting of the sun, is a beautiful specimen of an artichoke head. To achieve this clarity, the dried seedhead was carefully manicured with tweezers to rid it of all the damaged or slightly discoloured "petals". Repeating the artichoke shape in miniature, there is a generous scattering of the corn and white daisy-like ever-lasting flowers, xeranthemum. The misty background, against which all the other material shows up clearly, is provided by the dried fluffy seedheads of old man's beard, contrasting sharply in texture with the hard, silvery honesty seedheads. Long, curving sprays of lamb's ear (stachys) introduce a different shape – clusters of white woolly leaves at intervals along a stem. The last of the dried materials with, as it happens, much the same formation, are the stems of lavender, looking dark and significant amongst so many neutral tones.

Finally, the pale brownness of the material preserved in glycerine. On the left there is a clutch of sweet chestnuts, round and spiky like huge, overgrown burrs, preserved together with the catkins on the twig, and behind them, and through the centre, sprays of glistening chocolate-coloured mahonia leaves.

Copper cooking ware, if used in the oven or on top of the stove, is heavy on maintenance because contact with heat quickly tarnishes the metal and it needs constant cleaning. If you use yours to hold dried plant material when it will never come into contact with water, cleaning will be cut to a minimum. However, your bargains might be in need of care and attention when you find them – indeed, the more tarnished they are the more likely you are to acquire them at bargain prices.

If copper has taken on a bluish green colour, it is most effectively cleaned with a paste of well-powdered chalk and methylated spirits. Rub on the paste, leave it until the spirit has evaporated and the chalk becomes dry again, then remove and polish with fresh finely powdered chalk. Damp spots on brassware can be removed and the metal restored with a mixture of powdered chalk and spirits of turpentine. Badly tarnished copper, not yet at the green stage, can be restored by rubbing with half a lemon dipped in salt. Wash the copper thoroughly, dry it well then polish with a soft cloth. This treatment has the advantage of removing stains without robbing the metal of the patina of age, such an attractive feature of old metalware.

To prevent further oxidation, you can lacquer both brass and copper so that the metal will stay as bright as it was when you last polished it. To do this, polish well, brush away any traces of polish in crevices or indentations and rub with a soft cloth. Apply brass lacquer, like varnish, with a camel-hair brush and put the article in a hot oven for a few moments to set, or follow the manufacturer's instructions.

As you restore or polish your pieces of old copper and brass, you might discover mottoes or, at the least, the maker's initials inscribed on them; or find, amusingly, that unsuitable repairs have been made in the course of time. This would not be surprising, because the travelling tinkers in the nineteenth century, who went from village to village and town to town offering their services, often repaired copper and brass with more enthusiasm than skill. But their cry, one of the Victorian cries of London, "Any pots or pans to mend?" is nostalgically evocative of the age; their work lives on and has preserved for us so many of the utensils we enjoy searching for today.

Chapter 13

Pot-Pourri

Making pot-pourri is a wonderfully romantic way of storing up memories of the fragrance, colour and beauty of a garden. Lifting the lid from a bowl of dried petals and leaves is like taking the stopper off a bottle of expensive scent; yet infinitely more personal, because you can make pot-pourri from your own favourite flowers and scented leaves, spices and oils. You can even keep the recipe, if you wish, a closely guarded secret, as our grandmothers often did.

There are two kinds of pot-pourri, made by what are known as the dry and the moist methods. The dry method could not be simpler. It is just dried petals and leaves, a sprinkling of spice–any spice–and a little fixative stirred together and left to mature.

But the moist method is the one with the romance and charm of ages past. A hand-written recipe from 1660 calls for ingredients long since disappeared from our shop shelves, but it is worth recording here for the poetic way it evokes the age when the large houses and castles had a Lady of the Pot-Pourri–surely one of the most sentimental and rewarding positions in the household.

> *"Take one pound of rose petals, spread out and sprinkle with salt. Leave for two days*
> *until the petals are like leather, and the colour will have faded a little. Put the petals*
> *and salt into a large jar and sprinkle with two ounces of oil of bergamot.*
> *Stir in two ounces of the powder of the orris root and one ounce of gum benzedrine.*
> *Add one ounce each of nutmeg, cinnamon and cloves, all powdered. Then one*
> *ounce of angelica root, a few drops of oil of musk, and leave for some days. Stir in*
> *thin slices of the peel of two lemons. Put a lid over all and leave for some more days,*
> *perhaps one month, stirring when you will."*

Just as we can find inspiration from early cookery books, so we can adapt recipes such as this and make use of ingredients we can buy now. The principle of making moist pot-pourri is to mix dried petals, flowers and leaves with common salt, add a fixative such as powdered orris root or gum benzedrine (both still available), spices and flower oils. The traditional pure extracts of musk, bergamot, lavender, jasmine, rosemary, thyme, violet and attar of roses are not easy to come by now; when you can find them in old-fashioned shops with an aura of nostalgia, they are expensive. However, we have experimented with a range of oil-based perfume essence. This gives excellent results and was pronounced by a pharmacist we consulted to be the purest flower oil he had tested in years. We even tried culinary essences such as lemon, vanilla and almond; you can use lemon juice and brandy, too. With the addition, in the moist method, of these oils and essences, it is not as important to choose petals and leaves for their fragrance, as this will be enhanced and enriched by the oils. You can, therefore, include in your mixture a high proportion of flowers, like larkspur florets and marigolds, pansies and nasturtium, chosen simply for their colour or shape.

Pot-pourri can be an on-going art and is by no means confined to summer flowers. You can dry the sweet-smelling spring flowers and store them in sealed polythene bags or lidded boxes ready to be blended with the summer blossoms as they come. As you add more flowers to your pot-pourri from time to time, add a little more orris root powder and spice, a few drops of flower oil or essence and bring your pot-pourri to life all over again.

Moist Pot-pourri, the modern way
You will need the equivalent of: 8 ounces flowers, leaves and herbs, mixed; 4 ounces common household salt; 2 ounces powdered orris root; $\frac{1}{2}$ ounce ground cinnamon; $\frac{1}{2}$ ounce ground allspice; $\frac{1}{2}$ ounce ground cloves; $\frac{1}{2}$ teaspoon grated nutmeg; thinly pared rind of 1 lemon and 1 small orange; 1 vanilla pod; flower oil or essence (see method); 1 teaspoon brandy (optional).

On a dry day, gather a total of 8 ounces of flower petals and heads, scented leaves and herbs. For their scent, choose fragrant red rose petals, picking them at their best before they are ready to fall, and a selection from summer jasmine, buddleia, carnation, rosemary flowers and lavender, and spring flowers such as wallflower, narcissus and hyacinth. For colour and shape, choose violets (which quickly lose their scent), pansies, marigolds and florets of larkspur and delphinium. Adapt this list to a well-balanced mixture of fragrance and colour from the flowers available, according to the season and what you have in your garden.

For the scented leaves, choose from bay, thyme, sage, marjoram, verbena, balm, bergamot, mint, rosemary, rose-scented and lemon-scented geranium leaves.

Strip the petals from large flowers and leave the small ones whole. Spread them on small box lids, each flower type separate, and leave in hot sun to dry. Bring indoors overnight and put in the sun again the next day. The flowers will dry at different rates, according to their size and moisture content. As each type dries, put into a lidded container or a tightly closed polythene bag. Strip the leaves from their stalks, shred the larger ones, spread on box lids or trays and dry in the same way. Although sun-drying is the most natural and successful way, you can dry the materials in an airing cupboard, keeping a close watch on them and bringing them out when they become as crisp as cornflakes. In very windy weather this method is obviously preferable. Do not try to hasten the process by drying in front of direct artificial heat, such as an electric fire. This will draw the fragrance from the plants.

When all the petals, flowers and leaves have dried, put them in a large earthenware container with a lid or a large lidded polythene bowl. Sprinkle the salt between each layer, stir well, cover and leave for 2–3 weeks, stirring occasionally. Then stir in the powdered orris root, ground cinnamon, allspice, cloves and nutmeg, the thinly pared lemon and orange rind, finely chopped, and the shredded vanilla pod. Lastly add 1 teaspoon of flower oils or essence, or culinary essence, depending on what is available where you live. We used Mary Quant Perfume Essence, which is sold in 0·13-fluid ounce bottles in a range of scents including honeysuckle, wistaria, Spring Blossom and Country Garden. For a luxurious touch, add 1 teaspoon brandy. Cover the jar again, shake well and leave to mature for a further 2–3 days.

When the pot-pourri is ready, put it into glasses, brandy balloons, pretty teacups or bowls—Chinese porcelain bowls are traditional. If the pot-pourri dries out, as it is likely to do, particularly if left uncovered in a centrally-heated room, sprinkle on a little more salt, flower oil or essence and stir well. It should be kept constantly moist.

Dry Pot-pourri

For the dry pot-pourri method, dry the petals, flowers and leaves as described and mix together with 4 ounces of powdered orris root, the fixative, and any of the spices suggested in the "moist" recipe—or with your own choice. Put into a covered container and leave for 2–3 weeks, shaking frequently, before putting into jars, scent bottles or bowls or sewing into sachets, dolly bags or tiny pillows.

If you like the idea of preserving a single scent, use the dry method. You simply dry the flowers or leaves, add a little spice for muskiness and orris root powder, the preservative.

A tangy geranium mixture is made with 2 handfuls each of rose-scented and lemon-scented geranium leaves. Snip off the stalks, dry the leaves in the sun or in an airing cupboard and crumble them gently in your hands so they break up but do not go to powder. Add 2 dessertspoons ground allspice, 1 teaspoon grated nutmeg and 1 ounce of powdered orris root.

To capture the scent of roses, take 4 handfuls of dried rose petals and 1 handful of dried mock orange blossom petals. Mix them together and add 2 ounces each of ground coriander seeds and powdered orris root and 1 dessertspoon of ground cinnamon. Mix well together.

Perhaps lavender bags are the best-known of all sweet-scented sachets, and, like pomanders, they can be hung in wardrobes or linen cupboards or put in drawers with lingerie and woollens. Pick the lavender heads just before they are fully in bloom. Gather them when the early morning dew has dried, but before the hot sun has drawn away some of the fragrance—morning coffee time seems to be about the best! Hang bunches of lavender upside down to dry; or stand in a little water. Lavender-coloured organdie or voile are the traditional materials to make lavender bags or you could follow our designs and make tiny sachets and cushions in patchwork, the design based on lavender-coloured triangles.

For those who would like to achieve the effect of a pot-pourri without the soothing therapy of preparing it, there is a chemical preparation which contains the effects of the flower oils such as lilac, violet, lily of the valley, orange blossom, rose, lavender, rosemary and others; spices from cinnamon to patchouli and frankincense, and fixatives including vetiver root and oakmoss, which

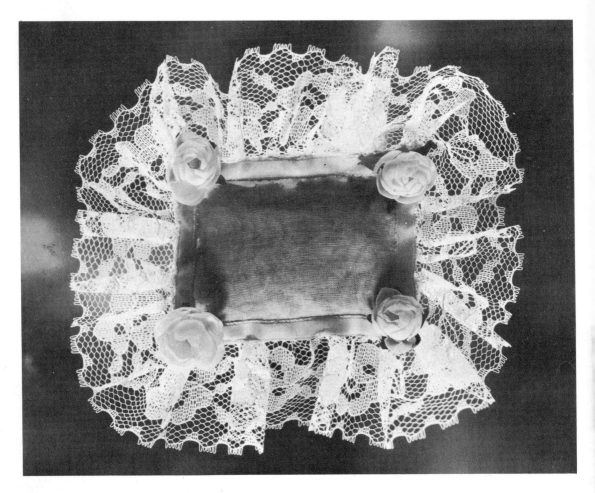

enhance and preserve the perfume. You simply have to add one measure of this pot-pourri maker to one quart of dried petals and leaves, shake thoroughly and leave for 2–3 weeks to mature. The petals retain their colour and whether they were scented or not in the first place, take on the combined aromas of this modern mix.

Pot-pourri pillows and sachets

In the nineteenth century, herb pillows were used as "softeners". At the first hint of an unkind remark, a glance out of place or any other sign that all was not well, a lady would turn her face to her herb pillow and look to it to soothe her jangled nerves. Herb pillows, or pot-pourri sachets tucked under a pillow, were used, too, to induce sleep – a less exhausting remedy for insomnia than counting sheep. Any pot-pourri made by the dry method, or single fragrances of dried lavender flowers or rose petals, are suitable to sew into tiny pillows, bags or sachets. For pillows and scatter cushions, choose lightweight cottons in romantic pastel colours or soft, spriggy floral prints, and for sachets – the kind you will tuck into the folds of your lingerie – muslin, voile, organdie, lawn or fine net. Our pillow designs are shown in colour on page 75 and the sachets on page 76.

112

A charming little pot-pourri sachet, only a few inches long, makes a pretty present and brings the scents of summer to handkerchiefs and lingerie.

Brown-flowered pillow and dolly bag

We chose a pale cream Liberty cotton lawn printed with brown flowers. Any fine cotton with a small, all-over flower design would be suitable.

For the pillow you will need: $\frac{1}{4}$-yard of 36-inch-wide (approximately 23 cm of 1-metre wide) fabric (this will, in fact, be enough to make two of the pillows and one dolly bag); 1 yard (1 metre) 1-inch (2·5 cm) wide coarse cream cotton lace; 24 inches (60 cm) $\frac{1}{4}$-inch (7 mm) wide pink baby ribbon; sewing thread.

For the dolly bag you will need: 9 inches (23 cm) coarse cream cotton lace; 30 inches (76 cm) $\frac{1}{4}$-inch (7 mm) wide pink baby ribbon; sewing thread.

To make the pillow, cut two $7\frac{1}{2}$-inch (19 cm) squares from the cotton. On all four sides, turn back and press a seam allowance of $\frac{1}{4}$-inch (7 mm). With right sides of the material together, machine round three sides and along one half of the fourth side, leaving an opening to fill the pillow with petals. Turn the pillow right side out. Cut diagonally across the corner of one end of the coarse lace, neatly turn in a narrow hem and stitch it down with matching thread. Beginning at one corner of the pillow, oversew the lace to the cotton fabric with small stitches. As you reach each corner, make a crease diagonally across the lace from the corner of the pillow to the top of the lace and fold so that the corner forms a neatly mitred right angle. Catch along the fold with a few stitches to secure before continuing to oversew along the next side. When you are attaching the lace to the fourth side, be careful not to oversew the opening. Finish the lace by cutting at an angle, taking a small hem and sewing it to the first corner.

Pack the pillow with dry pot-pourri, using enough petals to give a well-rounded appearance, but not so many that they will be crushed to powder. Oversew the opening. Cut a 15-inch (36 cm) length of the narrow ribbon, tie into a bow with long, trailing ends and sew in the centre of one edge of the pillow.

To make the dolly bag, cut a piece of cotton 9 by $4\frac{1}{2}$ inches (23 by 11·5 cm). Press $\frac{1}{4}$-inch (7 mm) seam allowance down the two long sides and press a 1-inch (2·5 cm) turning on each of the two short sides. Machine two rows of stitching, just over $\frac{1}{4}$-inch (7 mm) apart, as a track for the threaded ribbon near the top of each of the short sides over the doubled up material. Sew the 1-inch (2·5 cm) lace on each end first, with the material on the right side. Then turn inside out and seam the edges, avoiding the spaces between the two rows of stitching forming the track. Turn right side out. Cut ribbon into two 15-inch (36 cm) lengths. Using a bodkin or large darning needle, thread one strip of ribbon through the track on each side. Stuff the bag with petals, draw the ribbons to close the top and tie in two bows. Stitch through each knot to secure. Cut the ends of the ribbon diagonally to prevent fraying.

Pink lacy pillow and heart-shaped cushion

The soft, romantic colours and the Valentine shape of the little cushion make this set a natural for musky red rose petals.

For the pillow you will need $\frac{1}{4}$-yard (23 cm) pink lightweight cotton fabric, 36 inches (approximately 1 metre) wide (again, enough to make two pillows and one cushion); 15 inches (36 cm) $2\frac{1}{2}$-inch (6 cm) wide cotton lace trimming; $7\frac{1}{2}$ inches (19 cm) 1-inch (2·5 cm) wide; 15 inches (36 cm) $\frac{1}{4}$-inch (7 mm) wide white scalloped lace; at least 1 yard (1 metre) $\frac{1}{2}$-inch (13 mm) wide lace trimming for the edging; sewing thread.

For the heart you will need: 4 inches (10 cm) 1-inch (2·5 cm) wide lace; 8 inches (20 cm) $\frac{1}{4}$-inch (7 mm) scalloped lace; at least $\frac{3}{4}$-yard (70 cm) $\frac{1}{2}$-inch (13 mm) lace for edging.

To make the pillow, cut two $7\frac{1}{2}$-inch (19 cm) squares of the cotton. Cut the 15-inch (36 cm) lengths of the widest and the scalloped lace in half. Turn under and press $\frac{1}{4}$-inch (7 mm) seam allowance on one piece of the pink cotton, for the top and bottom edges. Lay the lace on the right side of the fabric, as shown in the photograph, in this order, working from the centre outwards: 1-inch (2·5 cm) wide lace in the centre, then, on each side of it, scalloped trimming and $2\frac{1}{2}$-inch (6 cm) wide lace. First tack and then hand sew or machine the lace in position. Now make up the cushion as previously described. Press $\frac{1}{4}$-inch seam allowances on second fabric square. With right sides together, machine along three sides and half of the fourth side; turn right side out.

For the edging, cut two 18-inch (46 cm) lengths of the $\frac{1}{2}$-inch (13 mm) wide lace. Take a running stitch, either by machine or by hand, along one long edge of each strip and gather up until each piece is just over 7 inches (18 cm) long. Turn in and stitch a narrow hem on each edge of the lace. Sew one strip by hand to each side of the cushion. Stuff the cushion with rose petals and oversew the opening.

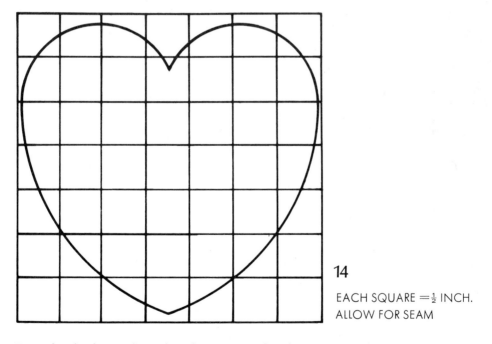

14

EACH SQUARE $=\frac{1}{2}$ INCH.
ALLOW FOR SEAM

To make the heart-shaped cushion, copy the shape in Diagram 14. Cut out two shapes from the pink cotton. On the right side of one piece of the cotton, place the 4-inch long strip of 1-inch (2·5 cm) wide lace vertically in the centre. Outline this strip on each side with the $\frac{1}{4}$-inch scalloped trimming. Tack in place and hand sew or machine. Press a scant $\frac{1}{4}$-inch (7 mm) seam allowance round the two heart shapes and, with right sides together, machine round the edges, leaving a small opening at one side. Push a pencil point into the point of the heart to get a well defined shape. Pack the heart with rose petals and oversew the opening. Gather up the remaining strip of $\frac{1}{4}$-inch (7 mm) wide lace until it is the right length to outline the heart shape.

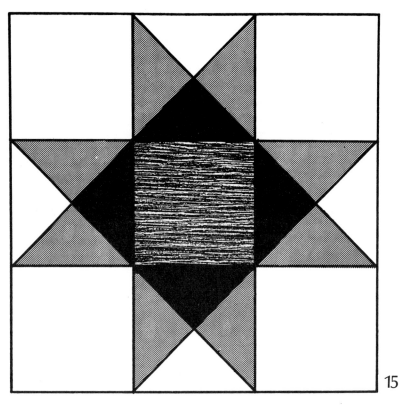

15

Patchwork pillows

A variation in the lavender bag theme, this pair of pretty patchwork pillows is made in lavender, pink and brown cottons trimmed with cream lace, and filled with sweet-scented lavender. The patchwork pattern, a traditional one, is called a variable star. It consists of five squares of equal size – the deep pink one in the centre and the paler pink ones at the corners – and four squares each made up of four triangles. For the larger pillow, the squares are $2\frac{1}{2}$ inches (approximately 6 cm) and for the miniature one, $1\frac{1}{8}$ inches (30 mm).

To make the pillows, you will need scraps of plain and patterned cottons, or silks, of equal weight. It is most important to choose all fine or all medium-weight fabrics as even the slightest difference in weight and thickness, when turned over the template, will alter the size of the patch and spoil the accuracy of the work. For the same reason, the fabric must be closely woven. Filmy, flimsy materials, or those with a stretchy open weave, are not suitable.

For this piecing method of patchwork, you cut a "template" or pattern for each patch, cut the fabric slightly larger all round than the card shape and tack the fabric firmly round the shape on all sides. The patches are joined together at the back, using overstitch and catching one or at the most two threads at a time. When all the sides of each patch have been sewn together, the tacking stitches and the templates can be removed. Patchwork is normally lined but this is not recommended for these scented pillows—the thicker the cover, the less fragrance will be released.

To avoid confusion, draw the design of each pillow to scale, marking in each square and triangle. Number the shapes and then number your postcard shapes accordingly. Iron all materials before cutting out.

Begin by cutting a master template for each shape using a steel rule for absolute accuracy. Trace two large squares and two small squares, from Diagram 15. Draw two diagonal lines across one square in each size to obtain the triangle template. Transfer these shapes on to card—old postcards are ideal—and cut out. Then using these shapes as your pattern and cutting out one at a time, cut a total of five squares and 16 triangles in each size.

To cut out each shape from the cotton, place the card template on the straight grain of the fabric. In the case of triangles, place the base line, that is to say the longest side, on the straight grain. Do not try to get more patches out of a scrap of fabric by turning shapes so that they are cut on the bias; they would stretch and pull out of shape. With a pencil, draw carefully and accurately round the template on the wrong side of the fabric. Cut out the shape with sharp scissors, allowing a turning all round of $\frac{3}{8}$-inch (10 mm) on the larger and $\frac{1}{4}$-inch (7 mm) on the smaller patches. When you are using materials with a floral or other design, move the template along until the main part of the design, a flower, motif or whatever, is centred on the patch—in the fabrics we have chosen, however, this is not applicable.

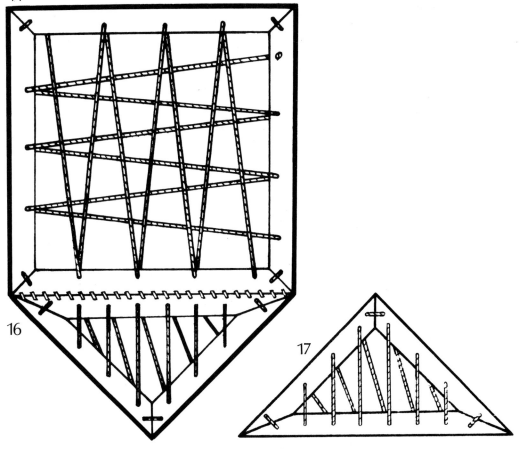

Position the template again on the wrong side of each patch, taking care to centre it accurately so that the seam allowance is equal all the way round. Bring the seam allowance over the template and secure by taking long stitches from top to bottom of the patch, pulling the thread so that the fabric is taut but not stretched. Mitre each corner neatly and oversew securely. Then take long stitches on the seam allowance from side to side of the patch until the template is completely enclosed in a network of stitches.

Diagram 16 shows this clearly. When working triangular patches, it might be necessary to snip a small piece away from each corner to achieve a neat finish. The narrow points of the triangles need particular care; do not worry too much about the appearance of the back of the work – slight "lumps" of turned over fabric are inevitable and will not show.

When you have tacked all the patches round the templates, begin sewing the patches together, following the numbered scale drawing you made of the design. Using a fine needle and thread, take tiny oversewing stitches at the back of the patches (Diagram 17). In this way, no stitching will be visible on the face of the work.

Snip out all the criss-cross tacking stitches and withdraw the templates when all sides of each patch are joined to the next – or when the piece is complete. Press the patchwork thoroughly under a damp cloth, opening out the seam allowances all round the edge of the square. You will then have one square approximately $8\frac{1}{4}$ inches (21 cm) and one $3\frac{7}{8}$ inches (10 cm). Cut squares of plain cotton for the backing in exactly the same sizes, making certain to have one side of each square on the straight grain. On the backing cotton, turn over and press seam allowances corresponding to those round the patchwork squares. Pin each patchwork piece to its backing cotton, right sides together, and then machine round three and a half sides. Turn right side out. Sew the narrow scalloped lace round all four sides of each pillow. Stuff the pillows well with lavender flowers to give a good, plump appearance. Neatly oversew the openings.

Pot-pourri sachets

The sachets shown in colour on page 76 are made in fine organdie, used double. Any fine sheer fabric would do equally well; scraps from an evening or bridal dress, or remnants of veiling, voile, lace or chiffon. The sachets can be made in any shape – round, oval, square, diamond, heart; the ones shown measure approximately 3 by 2 inches (7·5 by 5 cm). The organdie was used double in each case. This not only gives more protection to the petals but an interesting texture which catches the light in different ways.

Besides the scraps of fine material, you will need approximately 1 yard (1 metre) of 1-inch (2·5 cm) wide scalloped and flowered lace for the trimming. Allow almost three times the perimeter of the sachet so that it can be luxuriously gathered. Then, enough $\frac{1}{4}$-inch (7 mm) wide satin ribbon to outline the shape – approximately 12 inches (30 cm); tiny artificial flowers, such as bridal rosebuds or guipure lace daises; sewing thread.

For each sachet, cut four pieces of organdie in the shapes you require. You can use a tin lid or a small box, perhaps, as a guide. Machine the four pieces together, allowing about $\frac{1}{4}$-inch (7 mm) for the seam allowance and leaving an opening for the filling. Turn right side out. Use an orange stick or small nail file to push out the corners of squares or diamonds. Machine or run a row of stitching along the bottom edge of the 1-inch (2·5 cm) wide lace and gather it up so that it is the same length as the perimeter of the sachet. Carefully sew it in position round the sachet, frilling out the corners, if any. Sew the ribbon in position all round, covering the bottom of the lace trimming. Turn any corners at an angle, or ease ribbon round circular shapes. Loosely fill the sachet with dry pot-pourri. Oversew the opening. Sew flowers in position over the ribbon.

The sachets make delightful mini gifts, tucked inside a greeting card or sent with a thank-you letter. And if you are giving a present of lingerie or a pretty blouse, a sachet tucked in the folds would be almost as welcome as the gift itself.

Tussie mussies

The subject of sweet-smelling herbs and flowers would not be complete without a mention of tussie mussies, the herb posies still traditionally carried into court by judges in England. Until the eighteenth century, these posies, like pomanders, were carried to ward off unpleasant smells and, it was thought, as a protection against infection.

The little nosegays can be made up of any combination of scented flowers, herbs and leaves, either fresh or dried (see colour photograph on page 93). Set in a small wine glass or pottery jar, they make an attractive decoration beside each place at a dinner party, a welcome surprise on a breakfast tray or a long-lasting floral decoration in front of the looking-glass on a dressing table.

They usually have a small, dried flower in the centre; nothing could be prettier than a tightly curled rosebud. There is something of the feeling of a Victorian posy about tussie mussies in the way that the herbs, leaves and other flowers, if any, are arranged in tight rings round the centre flower. Strong contrast in both texture and colour is important.

Silvery green feathery leaves, such as artemisia or centaurea maritima, for example, could be encircled by lemon verbena or mint; then spiky leaves again, perhaps rosemary or lavender, and an outer layer of rose- or lemon-scented geranium leaves, sage or young bay leaves. If fresh herbs are used and the posies left undisturbed, the leaves will dry and retain their scent. It is best to dry the rosebud first in a chemical preparation (see Chapter 2).

The tussie mussies featured in the colour photograph on page 93 contain some of the traditional flowers and herbs, and others which we thought effective. The containers are simple glass spice jars, each given a collar of non-hardening modelling clay pierced with holes to take the stalks. Another way of doing it would be to wire each posy into a bunch and stand it to rest on top of the jar.

1. A white lawn daisy in the centre, turned pale lime green after drying in desiccant, is surrounded by dried red and pink daisies. Outlining the flowers, white latifolia, then thyme and rosemary.

2. Another daisy-type flower, ringed by sprigs of thyme, deep purple lavender, and four pale green Bells of Ireland heads. The outer layer is bay leaves coaxed to lie almost flat.

3. Pale grey lavender leaves cluster round the central feature, a coral rosebud dried in desiccant. After that, pale mauve lavender flowers and bay leaves set almost upright, giving a quite different perspective. This is also shown in the picture opposite.

4. Three white daisies faded to greeny yellow, dried primula and forsythia, with pale grey lavender leaves, thyme and an outer hoop of green Bells of Ireland.

Chapter 14

Dried Flower Delicacies

If, while you are preserving your plant material, you feel like a cup of tea, you will have a wide choice right there in front of you. For the fresh or dried leaves, flowers and seeds of many herbs and other plants can be infused in boiling water to make a refreshing tisane.

These infusions have their origins long before tea was imported from India, Ceylon and China—and were popular long after too, for the imported leaves were so very expensive. Tisanes were accredited by their devotees with many healing powers and were taken in good faith as aids to digestion, headaches, catarrh, colds, nervous disorders, insomnia and fatigue—for just the same reason that a nice cup of tea is offered today.

The general rule when making herbal teas is to allow one teaspoon of dried herbs or three teaspoons of fresh herbs for each cup and, in each case, an extra one "for the pot". They can be made just as ordinary tea. First warm the pot, add the seeds, flowers or crumpled leaves, pour on boiling water and leave to infuse from 5–15 minutes. You can use a teapot, a jug or a cup; the infusion will need straining before serving. If sweetening is needed, honey and not sugar is usually added. Part of the beauty of these teas is in the gradual deepening and strengthening of a colour which is never more than delicate. And so, for the colour photograph of camomile tea on page 94, we chose a glass teapot; the dried flowers are held in a glass filter suspended underneath the lid. Here are the directions for making a few of the most popular herb teas.

Angelica Tea Use only fresh, young leaves, in the proportion recommended above—

three teaspoons for each cup, plus one extra. Infuse for 5 minutes before straining and serving.

Basil Tea Use fresh or dried leaves; serve hot, or cold with an ice cube and a sprig of the fresh herb.

Bergamot Tea Use either fresh or dried leaves; add 1 heaped teaspoon dried leaves when making a pot of China tea.

Borage Tea Use dried flowers. One heaped teaspoonful to 1 pint ($2\frac{1}{2}$ cups or 0·56 litre) of boiling water.

Camomile Tea (photograph on page 94) Use the dried flowers. If you do not grow them, you can buy them from some chemists or herbalists. Allow about 30 dried flowers to 1 pint ($2\frac{1}{2}$ cups or 0·56 litre) of boiling water. Infuse for 15 minutes. Sweeten, if at all, with honey. Camomile has a varied fan club: Brer Rabbit liked it; Talleyrand expressed himself very partial to camomile tea, and it was a favourite of Queen Adelaide!

Clover Tea Use dried flower heads. One teaspoon for each cup. The red clover, which is the State flower of Vermont, makes an especially delicate tisane.

Marshmallow Tea Use dried flowers. The infusion is an attractive sugar-almond pink and has one of the most delicate flavours.

Meadowsweet Tea Use fresh or dried leaves and flowers. Gerard wrote: "The flowers and leaves of Meadowsweet farre excelle all other strowing herbs . . . for the smell thereof makes the heart merrie and joyful and delighteth the senses."

Nettle Tea Use dried flowers of the white nettle. Allow slightly less than the usual 1 teaspoon per cup. The flavour is stronger than most.

Orange Blossom Tea Use dried orange blossom, a teaspoon to a cup. Sweeten with orange flower honey.

Tansy Tea Use dried flowers and leaves in the usual quantities.

Violet Tea Use dried flowers, a teaspoon to a cup. Violet tea was a favourite of the Duchess of Kent, mother of Queen Victoria, and was often served in the Royal drawing rooms. Illinois, New Jersey, Rhode Island and Wisconsin all have the violet as their State flower.

Yarrow Tea Use fresh leaves and flowers.

Herb flowers and leaves can be infused in vinegar or in oil, too. They give a distinctive flavour which will make a subtle but important difference to salad dressings, sauces and marinades. Flowers infused in syrup or in dry sugar give the opportunity to add a range of delicate flavours to puddings and confectionery. And, incidentally, flowers or petals covered in sugar emerge dried; the sugar draws out both the moisture and the aroma. The following suggestions will give a general guide to the basic principles and ideas for adaptation with the herbs and flowers you can find. We have photographed them on page 95.

Burnet Vinegar Dry the seeds of salad burnet. Grind $\frac{1}{2}$-ounce (about 2 tablespoons or 14 g) dried seed in a mortar. Pour 1 quart (40 fluid ounces or 1·3 litre) warmed red or white wine vinegar over the seed and transfer into a bottle. Tightly cork the bottle and leave in a warm place for 10 days, shaking daily. Strain through filter paper or doubled muslin and discard the seed. Transfer the vinegar to a fresh bottle and keep tightly corked. The vinegar is a welcome addition to dressings for green salads, especially chicory. In Italy, where burnet is called Pimpinella, there is a saying:

"The salad is neither good nor fair,
 If Pimpinella is not there."

Coriander and Dill Vinegar can be made with the seeds in the same way.

Peach Blossom Vinegar Dry peach blossom that has been blown from the tree. Take about 1 ounce (28 g) dried flowers. Pour on 1 pint (0·56 litre) warmed vinegar, transfer to a bottle and cover tightly. Stand in a warm place, preferably on a sunny windowsill, for at least 14 days. Taste. If the flavour has not penetrated the vinegar sufficiently, repeat with more dried blossoms. Strain into another bottle and cover.

This method can be used with dried blossoms of other fruit trees. The flower vinegars have a delicate flavour and are particularly good when making pavlova or in dressings for green salad.

Tarragon and other Herb Vinegars Use fresh herb leaves. Infusing in vinegar is, indirectly, a way of preserving the leaves in near-fresh condition. Gather the leaves on a dry day and, in the case of flowering herbs, just before the plants come into full bloom. Allow about 2 cups of leaves to each 1 quart (40 fluid ounces or 1·3 litre) of vinegar. White or red wine vinegar is best for tarragon, marjoram, summer savory and basil. Use cider vinegar or distilled vinegar for mint, lemon balm and borage. Malt vinegar can be used, but gives a "rounder" result. Wash and dry the leaves and pack them into a wide-necked glass jar, with a ground-glass stopper or screw top. Pour in the vinegar and cover. When using fresh leaves, do not warm the vinegar. Cover the jar and leave it in a warm or sunny place for about 10 days. Shake or stir daily. Strain away the herbs and funnel the vinegar into bottles and cork tightly. For extra flavour and effect you can add a sprig of the appropriate fresh herb.

Rose Vinegar Fill a jar with red damask petals and press them well down. Cover with white wine vinegar. Cover jar and leave in a warm place for about a month, shaking or stirring every two or three days. Strain the vinegar, pour into bottles and cork. Alternatively, use about 1 cup dried damask rose petals and 1 pint (20 fluid ounces or 0·56 litre) warmed white vinegar. Rose vinegar gives piquancy to fruit syrups, particularly fruit salad, and can be used in salad dressings or Turkish dishes.

Rosemary Vinegar Use the dried flowers. Take 2 heaped teaspoons, add 1 pint (20 fluid ounces or 0·56 litre) warmed vinegar, transfer to a bottle and cover tightly. Leave in a warm place for at least 14 days, shaking daily. Strain, transfer to a fresh bottle and keep corked.

Herb Oils Infusions of herbs in edible oils such as olive, sunflower or corn oil must not be confused with the plant oil extracts used in making pot-pourri (Chapter 13). To make herb oil use fresh herb leaves in the proportion 2 heaped tablespoons to ½-pint (10 fluid ounces or 280 ml) oil. Pound the leaves in a pestle and mortar, or put them in a blender. Put the herbs and oil in a 1-pint (half-litre) bottle (it is important that the container should be no more than three-quarters full). Add 1 tablespoon of wine vinegar. Cork the bottle and stand it in strong sunlight – on a south- or east-facing windowsill – for between two and three weeks, shaking it at least twice a day. Sunlight has a very beneficial effect on herb oils, so try to be your own meteorologist and start them at the beginning of a heat-wave. If you strike a bad patch of weather, stand the bottles in a little water in the top of a double boiler and heat gently for a few hours each day for a week.

Strain the herbs from the oil, crushing all the moisture from the leaves. Add a sprig of fresh herb to each bottle and store tightly corked.

Herb oils using basil, fennel, rosemary, tarragon and thyme are invaluable in all kinds of dishes. Besides the obvious salad dressing and marinades, they can be used when preparing poultry, meat and fish casseroles, in the batter mixture for vegetable fritters and in sauces.

A bunch of herbs, known as **bouquet garni,** is a practical way to add a blend of aromas and enhances the flavour of casseroles, soups, stews and sauces. Traditionally, the bouquet consists of a bay leaf and a sprig each of marjoram, parsley and thyme. For convenience, the bouquet can be tied up in a small square of muslin, or sewn into a tiny sachet or bag, just as one makes lavender bags. It is easy, then, to remove the herbs before serving a dish. A box of these tiny sachets, offering the fragrance of your garden, would make a most welcome gift for an enthusiastic cook.

Rose Water is often called for in pudding, ice cream and syrup recipes. Again, it is not very easy to buy, but with a bed of red damask roses (or, indeed, any scented roses) in the garden, you can easily make it. Pick the roses before the petals start to drop. Pull off the petals and fill them to the top of a fireproof pan or casserole. Push the petals well down with the back of a spoon and fill up the vessel with water. Bring to simmering point without allowing to boil. Maintain this temperature for about an hour. Strain off the petals and replace with fresh petals. Simmer for a further hour, strain and bottle. Keep tightly corked under refrigeration.

Rose Syrup Put 1 pint (20 fluid ounces or 0·56 litre) of warm rose water into a pan, add 2 lb (900 g) of caster sugar and stir over gentle heat until the sugar has dissolved. Add 1 tablespoon lemon juice. Pour into bottles, cork tightly and keep in the refrigerator. The syrup can be poured over sweet pastries, added to whipped cream as a filling for meringues and used in ice creams and numerous other puddings.

Camomile Syrup Use dried camomile flowers. Put 4 ounces of flowers in a jar, add 3 pints (60 fluid ounces or 1·7 litre) of boiling water and cover. Allow to stand for 8 hours, stirring occasionally. Strain through filter paper or doubled muslin. Pour into a pan, add 3 lb (1·35 kg) granulated sugar and stir over low heat until sugar has dissolved. Bring to the boil and boil rapidly for 10 minutes. Cool, bottle and cover. Keep under refrigeration.

Poppy Syrup is made in the same way. Use 4 ounces dried poppy petals to $2\frac{1}{2}$ pints (50 fluid ounces or 1·4 litre) of water. After filtering, add 3 lb (1·35 kg) granulated sugar.

Rose Petal Sugar Use dark red rose petals, gathered on a dry day. Pack them loosely into a wide-necked jar and fill the jar with caster sugar, packing to within $\frac{1}{2}$-inch (13 mm) of the rim. Cover the jar and leave for 8 days, stirring daily. Pour the sugar through a sieve to remove the petals and spread it on a baking tray. Dry in a very low oven and store in an airtight container.

Rosemary Sugar Wash and dry a handful of rosemary sprigs. Place in a jar and fill with caster sugar to within $\frac{1}{2}$-inch (13 mm) of the rim. Cover the jar and shake or stir well. Leave for 6–8 days, shaking or stirring daily. Remove the rosemary sprigs. Use the sugar in egg custards and sweet puddings.

Bay Sugar and Lavender Sugar can be made in the same way, with sprigs of bay leaves and sprigs of lavender leaves and flowers. Pick the lavender before the seeds ripen.

Mint Sugar This is a way of preserving mint in sugar and results in "instant" mint sauce; you simply mix equal parts of mint sugar, boiling water and vinegar. Wash, drain and dry the mint leaves. Strip from the stalks and chop finely. Fill a jar with alternate layers of chopped mint and sugar, finishing with sugar. Cover the jar and leave for 5–6 days when the mint sugar will be ready to use. Keep covered.

Parsley Honey If ever a clump of parsley has gone to seed almost overnight, without your noticing it, here's a way to turn it to advantage. Pick a handful of long stems, complete with leaves and seeds. Wash them and put them into a saucepan. Add water barely to cover, bring to the boil and simmer for 30 minutes. Strain through a jelly bag. For each 1 pint (20 fluid ounces or 0·56 litre) of water add 1 lb (453 g) granulated sugar. Stir over gentle heat until the sugar has dissolved, then boil rapidly until setting point is reached. To test this, put a teaspoon of the liquid on to a cold saucer and allow to cool. Push a finger along the surface. If it wrinkles, the honey is ready. Pour into clean, warm jars and cover with waxed paper and Cellophane covers.

Pickled Rosebuds Pick small, tightly furled rosebuds on a dry day. Wash and place in a wide-necked jar. Fill the jar with a mixture of one part granulated sugar to four parts white wine vinegar. Seal the jar with melted paraffin wax. Store in a dark place for about 4 weeks. Use the pickled rosebuds in salads; they are especially good mixed with cream cheese as fillings for sandwiches and pancakes.

Candied Flowers One of the gentlest, most delicate ways to preserve the spring and summer blossoms from your garden is to "candy" the flowers as shown in the photograph on page 96. They can be served as sweetmeats after dinner or used to decorate cakes, ices and cold desserts.

Choose flowers in a variety of shapes and colours. Not all flowers are edible so check before you start. We suggest violets, primroses, rose petals and rosebuds, cowslips, narcissi, forget-me-nots, daisies, heather and the blossom of almond, plum, apple, cherry, pear and peach trees. Be sparing when you pick the blossoms, though; remember that you are sacrificing a fruit for a crystallised flower.

Put 1 ounce (28 g) gum arabic crystals into a bottle and cover with rose water or orange flower water. Cover and leave for at least 24 hours, shaking frequently. When the crystals have dissolved, tip the solution into a bowl. Using a fine camel-hair paintbrush, carefully paint each flower or petal so that it is completely covered. Be sure to work the solution right inside the whole flowers, and over both sides of petals. Tweezers are useful to hold the flowers while you work. Sprinkle the flowers or petals with caster sugar (or rose sugar), again making sure that they are well covered. Shake off any loose sugar. Spread out on sheets of greaseproof and dry in a warm, dry place such as an airing cupboard. Store in an airtight tin between layers of greaseproof paper.

Another method, though it is more subject to atmospheric conditions such as high humidity and therefore slightly less reliable, is to brush the flowers and blossoms with unbeaten egg white. Sprinkle them with granulated sugar and leave to dry. Store in an airtight tin.

Preserved Angelica Cut young angelica stems; trim them to equal lengths. Boil the stems until tender. Remove from water and strip off outer skin. Return to pan and simmer slowly until the stems turn green. Dry well. To each 1 lb (453 g) of angelica, allow 1 lb (453 g) granulated sugar. Lay the stems in a dish and sprinkle with the sugar. Leave for 2 days then boil the sugar and stems together. Remove the stems, add a further 2 ounces (56 g) of sugar to the syrup and boil again. Add the angelica and reboil for a further 5 minutes. Drain the angelica. Spread it on a baking tray and leave in a cool oven to dry. Store in an airtight container. The angelica will provide the stems and leaves for decorations using the candied flowers.

HERBS AND BEAUTY

Greater awareness of our environment, talk about ecology and the interest in natural foods have started to turn back the clock. Old-fashioned and even ancient cosmetic recipes are now being sold alongside mass-produced preparations, and with their fresh-as-a-bright-spring-day aura they make us feel cosseted and cherished, in a purely natural way.

Many of these preparations are easy to make at home; looking round the garden or out on a country walk you will have come across many of the herbs used to scent oils and creams, to lighten or darken hair, soothe dry or tired skin and generally make you feel more beautiful.

Indeed, the tisanes described earlier in this chapter are ideal bath preparations. About a cupful of any of the herbal infusions will scent the bath and give you a languorous feeling of luxury. Herb oils, too, can be added to bath water. Even a few drops will make the very steam carry the fragrance, and be a gentle treatment for a dry skin. You can add flowers and herbs in other ways: scatter a handful of rose petals, herb leaves or rose- or lemon-scented geranium leaves on the water. It's a rather lovely feeling to have them float by you. Experiment with any scented flowers or leaves you like, but avoid mint; it tends to smell more medicinal than cosmetic in these circumstances. Camomile, lavender and, perhaps best of all, elder flowers are exquisite. Hang a muslin bag filled with lavender flowers or a mixture of herbs under the shower spray. This will be quite enough to scent the room.

Be your own cosmetician and add a few drops of herb oil to an unperfumed cold cream, or simply pound some leaves in a mortar and pestle to extract the juice and blend it with the cream. Pat your face with an infusion of nettles; it is a refreshing and mild astringent. Rinse blonde hair in camomile tea to bring out the highlights, brown or auburn hair in rosemary tea to strengthen the colour. And for a soothing face pack, stir crushed elder flowers into natural yoghourt.

Making your own cosmetics, simply and naturally, is a beautiful way to use the flowers and leaves from your garden.

Craft shops

Arts and Crafts
10 Byram Street
Huddersfield HD1 LDA

Cass Arts
216 – 218 The Marlowes
Hemel Hempstead
Herts HP1 1BH

Also at
18 George Street
Richmond
Surrey

Craft Technique
19 Old Orchard Street
Bath

Dryad Ltd
Northgates
Leicester LE1 4OR

Also at
178 High Street
Kensington
London W8

Leisurecraft Centre
Search Press Ltd
123 Falcon Road
London SW11

Index